SIDE DISHES
Creative and Simple

SIDE DISHES
Creative and Simple

Vegetable and Fruit Accompaniments
for All Occasions

DEIRDRE DAVIS

Illustrations by Callie Butler

CHAPTERS™

CHAPTERS PUBLISHING LTD., SHELBURNE, VT 05482

Published by Chapters Publishing, Ltd., 2085 Shelburne Road, Shelburne, VT 05482

Library of Congress Cataloging-in-Publication Data

Davis, Deirdre.
    Side dishes creative and simple: vegetable and fruit accompaniments for all occasions / by
Deirdre Davis; illustrated by Callie Butler.
    p.   cm.
    Includes index.
    ISBN 1-57630-027-7 (softcover)
    1. Cookery (Vegetables). 2. Cookery (Fruit) 3. Side dishes (Cookery)
    I. Title. II. Title: Side dishes creative and simple.
TX801.D287 1997
641.6' 5—DC21   96-37468

Printed in U.S.A. by
R.R. Donnelley & Sons

Designed by Susan McClellan

This book is dedicated to
my ten-year-old son, Max,
who has been very patient
and most willing to lend
a helping hand.

Acknowledgments

IF ANY ONE FEELING were to characterize the making of this book, it would be frustration. It seemed to me as though I went in fits and starts, moving along productively and energetically, only to be frozen by my own lack of creativity and external circumstances. Throughout it all, many people have been present, whispering, "Keep going." I am delighted to have the opportunity to send a huge thank you to all of them:

My three men: son Max Cullen, friend Kevin Cordima and father Russell Davis for their constant understanding as well as critical tasting. I am also grateful to Kevin for computer advice and support.

My family: Henry, Joan, Russell, Chris and Owen Davis; Kelly and Amelia Davis; Patty Davis and Jack Swig; and Geoff, Yami, Linc, Ali, Russ and Margie Davis for food discussions, gentle prodding when needed and lots of laughs.

Linda Marino, my very special friend, confidante and colleague, for her continual advice—both technical and personal—and most important, for her friendship.

Deborah Moules and her family Brandon Boyd and Sienna Boyd, my close friends and daily support.

Mariette and Robert Fitzgerald, lifelong friends.

My women's group for its solace, and the friendships of Marnie Malarkey, Tess Hopper, Jan Lindsay and Lisa Batchelder, whose sustenance and encouragement is indescribable.

My neighbors Sheila, Bob, Mark and Amanda Bodwell, who once again helped with countless tasting sessions and gave me wonderful feedback.

Laurie Hershberg, who spent many hours bolstering me as well as reading and struggling through the manuscript.

Kathy Gunst, Naomi Cottrell, Drew Spangler, Richard Kzirian, Tricia Schott, the Cordima Family, Suzy and David Auger, Tom Cordima and Debbie Coull, Oliver Coolidge and Nancy Thompson, and Nancy Klavans—friends and colleagues whose support, ideas and palates helped shape this book.

My agent, Doe Coover, who has tremendous insight and a sixth sense about the food and cookbook world.

My editor, Rux Martin, at Chapters, for believing in me and my ideas as well as giving me the room to cultivate my style.

Finally, my aunt, the late Judge Catherine B. Kelly, whose strength I aspire to and whose endorsement of my work has been an ever-present support.

Contents

Introduction

PEOPLE OFTEN TELL ME how tired they are of the same old rice with a pat of butter, plain boiled carrots or a humdrum baked potato. It doesn't have to be that way. For me, side dishes are the most exciting part of the plate, never an afterthought. You can easily add a squeeze of lemon juice and a few diced tomatoes to the rice. Toss some garlic cloves and black olives into the carrots. Make a quick topping of pinto beans with cumin and sour cream for the baked potato. With a single change, a dull plate-filler becomes a memorable new accompaniment.

Most of my inspirations for side dishes come from my local supermarket, where, whatever the time of year, an ingredient snatches my attention and triggers an idea. I buy what is available, as long as it is fresh, and then I let my imagination run. One day, it's red cabbage that catches my eye, tempting me to braise it with a few dried pears. On another day, the sight of a pile of gleaming celery prompts me to make a simple salad of steamed stalks, dressed with lemon juice, olive oil and some snappy capers and dill.

OFTEN, I SET OUT WITH A CERTAIN TEXTURE IN MIND. When I want a soft side dish, I may prepare mashed potatoes, mixing in sweet garlic puree; or I may braise cauliflower or squash until it melts in the mouth. At other times, especially in the summer months, I want crunch. I marinate cucumbers in vinegar, basil and mint and serve them icy cold. For contrast, I mix some toasted nuts into creamy risotto or top a hill of mashed potatoes with crispy fried garlic.

Classic recipes provide a wellspring of possibilities for the side of the plate. Few things are easier than ripe tomatoes gently stewed with butter and onion or scalloped potatoes baked with cream. I often reinterpret a traditional favorite and wind up with something completely new. Using gazpacho, the cold Spanish soup, as a jump-off point, I create a salad dressing for cooked dried beans. The ingredients of stuffed grape leaves—onions, pine nuts, raisins, lemon juice and mint—work just as well transposed into risotto.

A natural-born innovator, I can't resist combining ingredients not normally found together. I sauté pear slices in butter, seasoning them generously with coarsely ground black pepper and a sprinkling of lemon zest. Or I enliven a casserole of thin-sliced potatoes and sautéed onions by layering them with cranberries for a hint of tartness. Other unexpected pairings prove surprisingly harmonious. Rhubarb and tarragon, for example, taste wonderful together.

While all the dishes in this book complement the main course, I often make a meal of several of them, serving Baked Tomatoes together with Wilted Greens and Two Spaghetti with Pesto, or Lentil Tabbouleh with Cold Stuffed Zucchini. Baked Basmati Rice with Cardamom Custard doubles as a versatile main course, and its creamy neutral color offers a pleasing contrast to the bright radishes, carrots, snow peas and summer squash in Vegetable Jardinière. On other days, a warming bowl of Braised White Beans with Fennel accompanied by Roasted Vegetables—red peppers, onions and mushrooms—is all I need.

WHATEVER ITS INGREDIENTS or country of origin, make sure your side dish is properly seasoned. Even with bold spices and herbs, salt is important for balance, for it heightens flavor and can perk up produce that is not at its peak. Taste as you go and adjust accordingly.

The following recipes are intended to be guides, not strict blueprints. If your market doesn't have zucchini, buy green beans. Can't find arugula? Substitute escarole or spinach. If you don't like rosemary, substitute thyme or savory or leave the herb out altogether. When you don't have bulgur in the house, make the same dish with couscous or quinoa. Some of my best side dishes were created after I abandoned my preconceived plan and gave myself up to the contents of the pantry.

Chapter One

Fruits

DURING MY CHILDHOOD and young adult life, fruit side dishes in my house never ventured beyond the standard cranberry sauce at Thanksgiving and the obligatory jarred applesauce alongside roast pork. Then one day, while sipping a glass of bottled cranberry-apricot juice, I dropped a few dried cherries into a pot of simmering cranberries. If Ocean Spray could experiment, why couldn't I? The ruby-garnet colors of the dish were breathtaking, and the sweetness from the cherries balanced the berries without obliterating their tartness. I served my sauce with roast pork instead of the mandatory turkey.

Elated by my success, I decided to explore further, sautéing pears until browned and caramelized outside and soft and juicy within, tucking them onto a plate alongside lamb. After that, I experimented with apples, halving them, covering them with crumbs, garlic and parsley and baking them. They proved to be the perfect accompaniment to chicken breasts bathed in cider-lemon sauce.

Considering the array of fruit available to us, it's surprising that side dishes like these are not more common. Fruits, after all, are just as versatile as vegetables—and perhaps even more so. Their colors are brilliant, their flavors intense. Their sheer variety opens up a new territory of accompaniments to brighten daily fare. The complex sweet, spicy and tart essence of fruit both completes and contrasts with the savory quality of meat, poultry, game, seafood and vegetarian dishes. And while we tend to think of poaching or baking as the sole preparation methods for fruits, they also lend themselves to a spectrum of techniques usually associated with vegetables: stewing, grilling and sautéing.

Unlike most vegetables, however, fruits have the unique ability to play a sweet or savory role with equal ease. Sweet-and-Sour Stuffed Apples places the apple in the side-dish realm by filling it with a mixture of crumbs, vegetables, raisins and vinegar. A salad of ripe peaches and tomatoes is incomparable alongside grilled chicken. Grilled bananas are remarkable accompaniments to barbecued meats. Pears may be savored in a casserole with spices, mustard and cream and enjoyed with pork. Sweetly stewed rhubarb makes a simple, old-fashioned side dish, and it is equally wonderful sautéed in butter and seasoned with herbs.

OTHER DISHES in this chapter take conventional approaches. Stewed Tomatoes is a thoroughly gratifying dish. Baked Tomatoes, another classic, is simply prepared and can accompany almost any main course.

Fruit side dishes are particularly appropriate companions to spicy foods, cleansing and cooling the palate. They balance rich meats and fish, such as duck, pork, bluefish, swordfish and salmon. At the same time, they can complement lean dishes, keeping the meal light, or starches, such as rice, grains and pasta. Each of the following recipes can be counted on to bring the sparkle of the unexpected to any meal—just as cranberry sauce once did.

FRUITS

Stewed Rhubarb *with* Tarragon

Serves 4 to 6

STEWED RHUBARB is such a favorite in our house that it marks the beginning of the season just as corn and the first fall apples signal theirs. This dish has a savory element; the addition of tarragon is a pleasing departure from more usual versions. Serve with ham, duck, pork, sausages, rich fish such as bluefish or salmon, or with Chinese food.

1½   pounds rhubarb, rinsed and trimmed
½   cup sugar
¼   cup water
2   tablespoons chopped fresh tarragon
      or 2 teaspoons dried
      Salt
      Lemon wedges (optional)

Cut the rhubarb into ½-inch slices and place in a medium nonreactive saucepan with the sugar, water, tarragon and a pinch of salt. Cover and bring to a boil, stirring, over medium-high heat. Uncover, reduce the heat to medium-low and simmer for 5 to 10 minutes, stirring occasionally, until soft and tender.

Transfer to a bowl and cool to room temperature. Serve at room temperature or chill. Garnish with lemon wedges, if desired.

Variations

* Add 1 teaspoon cinnamon with the tarragon.
* Replace the tarragon with thyme or chives.

Grilled Bananas

Serves 4 to 8

WARM BANANA HALVES topped with a spicy butter blended with molasses and cocoa is a stellar match for marinated and grilled foods, such as pork tenderloin, pork chops, chicken, turkey breast or shellfish. It's also a terrific go-along with any rice dish. This recipe is loosely based on one from Chris Schlesinger and John Willoughby's *Thrill of the Grill* (William Morrow, 1990).

3 tablespoons unsalted butter, softened

2 tablespoons molasses (any kind)

1 teaspoon unsweetened cocoa

¼ teaspoon chili powder

   Salt

   Freshly ground black pepper

   Pinch of cayenne pepper

4 large firm bananas (do not peel)

   Oil with little flavor, such as safflower or vegetable

Prepare the grill by lighting the coals.

Place the butter, molasses, cocoa, chili powder, ¼ teaspoon salt, pepper and cayenne in a small bowl. Cream together with a fork until completely mixed and homogenous. Set aside to allow the flavors to blend.

When the coals are ready (there should be no flames, just glowing red coals with a layer of gray ash around them), cut the bananas in half lengthwise. Brush the bananas with oil on both sides and place them on the grill, 6 to 8 inches from the coals. Grill the bananas until softened, 2 minutes per side.

When the bananas are done, transfer them to a platter. Taste the butter mixture for spiciness and seasonings, adding more cayenne, salt and pepper if desired. Dot the bananas with the butter mixture and spread it with a knife over the surface to coat. Serve the bananas warm, still in their peels.

Grilled Spicy Pineapple

Serves 4 to 6

THIS SLIGHTLY SPICY PINEAPPLE is cooked until caramelized outside and just warmed through. The heat of the sauce from the cayenne pepper intensifies upon standing; taste and add more, if you like, just before spooning over the pineapple. Serve with all types of pork or chicken dishes.

    1 large pineapple (4-5 pounds)
   ¼ cup fresh lemon juice
   2 tablespoons honey
   ⅛ teaspoon cayenne pepper, or to taste
   2 tablespoons olive oil

Prepare the grill by lighting the coals.

To peel the pineapple: Lay the pineapple on its side and cut a slice off the top and the bottom. Stand it up on end and remove the peel, cutting in long slices from top to bottom. Trim any remaining "eyes," and place the pineapple back on its side.

Cut crosswise into 8 round slices; set aside.

Combine the lemon juice and honey in a small nonreactive saucepan and heat just to melt the honey. Pour into a small bowl and add ⅛ teaspoon cayenne. Set aside.

When the coals are ready (there should be no flames, just glowing red coals with a layer of gray ash around them), brush the pineapple slices lightly with the oil. Place the slices on the grill, 6 to 8 inches from the coals. Grill the slices until brown and warmed through, 2 to 3 minutes per side.

Arrange the pineapple slices on a platter or plates. Taste the lemon-honey mixture and add more cayenne, if desired. Spoon over the warm pineapple slices.

Melons and Cream

Serves 6

IN THIS COOLING DISH, coconut milk and vanilla match the perfume of the melons, with mint providing a refreshing finish. Arrange in a bowl, garnished with mint sprigs or on a bed of mixed greens. Serve with marinated and grilled chicken breasts, grilled pork tenderloins, grilled shrimp or a platter of Italian antipasto meats, such as prosciutto or salami.

¼ cup sour cream or drained yogurt (see page 114)

1 tablespoon oil with little flavor, such as safflower or vegetable

1 tablespoon fresh lime juice

1-2 tablespoons unsweetened coconut milk

1½ teaspoons vanilla

1 tablespoon chopped fresh mint or 1 teaspoon dried, crumbled

1 teaspoon sugar

Salt

Freshly ground black pepper

Pinch of cayenne pepper (optional)

1 ripe medium cantaloupe (about 3 pounds)

¼ pound spinach, stemmed, washed, dried and torn into pieces (optional)

1 small head Boston or Bibb-type lettuce, washed, dried and torn into pieces (optional)

Mint sprigs for garnish (optional)

Place the sour cream or yogurt in a small bowl. Add the oil, lime juice, 1 tablespoon of the coconut milk and vanilla; mix gently to combine. Add the mint, sugar, ⅛ teaspoon salt, some pepper, and cayenne, if using. Whisk gently to combine, and taste the sauce. Add the remaining 1 tablespoon coconut milk, if desired, and set aside in the refrigerator while you prepare the cantaloupe.

Cut the cantaloupe into 1-to-1½-inch wedges; seed and peel. Cut the wedges crosswise into ¼-inch-thick slices. Pile the slices in a medium bowl. Whisk the sauce and pour over the cantaloupe. Toss and marinate for 1 to 2 hours.

When ready to serve, mix the spinach and lettuce, if using, and place on a platter. Arrange the cantaloupe and sauce over the greens and serve. Alternatively, you can serve the cantaloupe in the bowl and garnish with mint sprigs, if available.

Variations

* Add 1 large minced garlic clove to the dressing for a more savory dish.

* Use this dressing on oranges, plums, mangoes or papayas, or on any combination of these fruits.

Peach and Tomato Salad

Serves 6

THIS UNUSUAL SALAD combines the voluptuous sweetness of peaches with the sweet-acid taste of tomatoes. Fennel contributes spiciness, and toasted hazelnuts add a welcome crunch. The salad is at its best when prepared with the juiciest fruit available at the peak of summer. If peaches are mealy, try substituting nectarines. For maximum flavor, you'll need to make up the fennel oil two days in advance. Serve with fish, chicken or pork, on a buffet or with focaccia and a few cheeses for a luncheon. This dish was inspired by a recipe in *Verdura* by Viana La Place (William Morrow, 1991).

¼ cup hazelnuts
4 large ripe peaches, yellow or white
4 medium-large ripe tomatoes
2 tablespoons fresh lemon juice
1 teaspoon fennel seeds, finely crushed

Salt
Freshly ground black pepper
¼ cup extra-virgin olive oil or fennel oil (recipe follows)
Fresh parsley, fennel, basil or mint sprigs for garnish

To toast the nuts: Preheat the oven to 350 degrees F. Spread the nuts in a cake pan and bake, stirring halfway through, for 10 to 15 minutes, or until lightly toasted. Remove from the oven.

To remove the skins from hazelnuts, wrap a clean dish towel around them and rub them together in the towel to loosen the skins; discard the skins. Chop the nuts and set them aside.

Cut each peach in half through the stem end and remove the pit. Place the peaches cut sides down and cut into ¼-inch-thick slices. Core and cut the tomatoes crosswise into ¼-inch-thick slices. Arrange the fruit on a platter, alternating the colors.

In a small bowl, whisk together the lemon juice, fennel seeds and a pinch each of salt and pepper. Slowly add the oil, whisking to blend. Taste and adjust seasonings.

Spoon the dressing over the fruit, scatter the reserved hazelnuts over the top and garnish the dish with the parsley, fennel, basil or mint.

Fennel Oil

Makes about 1 cup

½ cup fennel seeds
1 cup extra-virgin olive oil

Crush the fennel seeds with a mortar and pestle or use a blender. Add the oil and blend to mix. Pour the mixture into a jar, cover and let it sit for 1 to 2 days, refrigerated, before using. Strain the oil, discard the seeds, and use the oil right away, or keep refrigerated and use within 2 weeks.

Sliced Tomatoes
with Grape-Mint Sauce

Serves 4

THIS LOVELY, UNEXPECTED combination features a salad of tomato slices topped with a dressing of pureed green grapes flavored with mint and lemon juice. Improbable-sounding, yes, but delicious with the play of tomatoes against the sweet grapes. The dressing was inspired by the medieval condiment verjus, the tart juice of unripe green grapes. I have added lemon juice to cut the sweetness of store-bought grapes. There is no fat in this dish, and the salad requires very little time to make. Serve with hot or cold chicken or fish.

1 cup seedless green grapes

1 tablespoon fresh lemon juice

¼ cup whole mint leaves

Salt

Freshly ground black pepper

4 lettuce leaves

4 medium-large ripe tomatoes,
cored and sliced ¼ inch thick

Place the grapes and lemon juice in a blender. Puree the mixture until smooth. Add the mint leaves, ¼ teaspoon salt and some pepper. Blend to chop the mint until the dressing is pale green.

Place the lettuce leaves on 4 plates, arrange the tomato slices over the lettuce, and sprinkle with additional salt and pepper, if needed. Spoon the sauce over the slices and serve.

Stewed Tomatoes

Serves 4 to 6

SAVE THIS DISH for when you have juicy, fully ripe tomatoes from the vine. Serve with roast chicken, pan-fried veal scallopini, roast leg of lamb or an omelet.

4 tablespoons unsalted butter
1 large onion, chopped
  Salt
  Freshly ground black pepper
4 pounds ripe tomatoes, cored and
    cut into wedges
1 teaspoon sugar (optional)

Melt the butter in a large nonreactive saucepan or Dutch oven over medium-high heat. Add the onion, sprinkle with a little salt and pepper and cook for about 5 minutes, or until the onion begins to lose its moisture and soften, stirring once or twice. Add the tomato wedges and the sugar, if desired. Toss and cover.

Cook for 15 to 20 minutes, stirring occasionally, until the tomatoes soften and release their juices. Uncover and cook for 10 minutes more to reduce the juices slightly. Correct the seasonings, adding more salt and pepper as needed. Serve warm or cold.

Variations

* Add some chopped green pepper and celery when sautéing the onion.

* These are delicious with a bit of minced garlic thrown in.

* Stew with a stick of cinnamon or a pinch of ground cloves.

* Any chopped fresh herb, such as basil, parsley, oregano, thyme, tarragon or marjoram, is a nice addition.

* Add some green beans to the tomatoes and stew both together.

* On a hot day, enjoy these tomatoes cold with a squeeze of lemon juice.

Baked Tomatoes

Serves 6

EASY TO PREPARE, this dish adds color to any meal. Simply halve the tomatoes, season with salt and pepper, top with a layer of flavored bread crumbs and bake. The result: a nice contrast of textures between the warm softened tomato and the crisp topping.

Baked green tomatoes have a lemony sweet-tart flavor and go well with fish or chicken. Baked red tomatoes can accompany just about anything but are especially good with grilled or pan-fried steaks or chops. Both can be served at room temperature.

- 1 cup fresh bread crumbs
- 2 tablespoons chopped fresh parsley
- 2 tablespoons chopped fresh basil or 2 teaspoons dried
- 1 teaspoon ground cinnamon Pinch of ground allspice
- ¼ cup olive oil
- 1 large garlic clove, minced Salt Freshly ground black pepper
- 3 medium-large ripe, firm tomatoes (about 8 ounces each); avoid soft or overripe tomatoes

Preheat the oven to 400 degrees F.

Place the crumbs in a small bowl and add the parsley, basil, cinnamon and allspice. Mix with a fork. Add the oil, garlic, ¼ teaspoon salt and some pepper. Mix thoroughly until all the crumbs are moistened with the oil. Set aside.

Lightly oil an 11-by-7-inch baking dish or other pan with sides. Core the tomatoes and cut in half crosswise. Arrange the tomato halves cut sides up in the oiled pan and sprinkle with additional salt and pepper. Divide the crumbs evenly over the 6 tomato halves; there should be a thick layer of crumbs.

Bake the tomatoes for 15 to 20 minutes, or until the crumbs have browned and the tomatoes are soft when gently squeezed around the circumference. Serve straight from the oven or at room temperature.

Variation

Baked Green Tomatoes

Serves 6

Use tomatoes with a blush of color. Hard, unripe, all-green tomatoes do not work in this dish.

1 cup fresh bread crumbs

2 tablespoons chopped fresh parsley
   or thyme

3 tablespoons unsalted butter, melted

2 teaspoons (loosely packed) grated
   lemon zest

   Salt

   Freshly ground black pepper

3 medium-large green tomatoes,
   cored and halved crosswise

Preheat the oven to 350 degrees F.

Place the crumbs in a small bowl and add the parsley or thyme, butter, lemon zest, ¼ teaspoon salt and some pepper to taste. Mix thoroughly with a fork.

Lightly oil an 11-by-7-inch baking dish or other pan with sides. Place the tomatoes cut sides up in the oiled pan, sprinkle with some salt and pepper and divide the crumbs evenly over the tomato halves.

Bake for 30 to 40 minutes, or until the crumbs have browned and the tomatoes have softened. Serve straight from the oven or at room temperature.

Gratin *of* Pears

Serves 6 to 8

THIS DISH IS REMINISCENT of the classic potato gratin of France, but it is made with pears and mustard instead of potatoes. Choose a firm pear that will hold its shape during cooking. If you want a subtle mustard flavor, use 4 tablespoons Dijon; if you are looking for a more assertive taste, use the larger amount. This makes a wonderful buffet dish because it retains its heat for a long time, complements many dishes and adds variety to the table. Serve with ham, roast turkey, pork, chicken, duck or rabbit.

4   slightly ripe pears, unpeeled
      (2-2¼ pounds), preferably Bosc
1   tablespoon unsalted butter
    Salt
    Freshly ground black pepper
4-6 tablespoons Dijon mustard
1½ cups heavy cream
2   teaspoons fresh thyme leaves or
      1 teaspoon dried
½   teaspoon ground mace
1   cup fresh bread crumbs

Preheat the oven to 325 degrees F.

Quarter the pears lengthwise; core and cut the quarters crosswise into ¼-to-⅓-inch-thick slices. Melt the butter in a large skillet over medium-high heat. Add the pears, season with a little salt and pepper, and toss to coat with the butter. Cook the pears for 5 minutes to soften slightly, tossing often.

Meanwhile, whisk the mustard and cream together in a small bowl. Add the thyme and mace and season to taste with salt and pepper.

Arrange half the pears in a 1½-quart baking dish. Pour half the cream mixture over the pears. Repeat, using the remaining pears and cream. Scatter the bread crumbs evenly over the top.

Bake the dish for 1 hour, or until the cream is bubbly and reduced, the pears are tender and the crumbs are golden. Remove from the oven, let rest 5 to 10 minutes so the dish sets up, and serve.

Variations

* Add sautéed leeks or onions to the dish in layers over the pears.

* Scatter crisped bacon on top before adding the crumbs.

* Substitute chopped fresh rosemary or crumbled dried rosemary for the thyme.

* Add 2 teaspoons grated orange zest to the mustard-cream mixture.

* Sauté 2 minced garlic cloves with the pears.

* Mix ½ cup toasted and chopped nuts to the crumbs, such as walnuts, almonds or pine nuts. To toast nuts, see page 22.

Sautéed Lemon Pears

Serves 4 to 6

IN THIS SIMPLE PREPARATION, pear slices are quickly browned in butter over high heat. When they are done, a good dose of grated lemon zest and ground black pepper is added, which blends with the butter and coats the pears like a sauce. I like to use firm, slightly ripe Bosc pears because they hold their shape well and retain just a bit of crispness. Serve this dish warm alongside pork chops or other pork dishes, lamb, poultry or game.

4 slightly ripe pears, unpeeled
  (2-2¼ pounds), preferably Bosc
4 tablespoons unsalted butter
  Salt
1 teaspoon (tightly packed) grated
  lemon zest
½ teaspoon coarsely cracked black
  peppercorns
  Juice of ½ lemon, or lemon wedges

Quarter the pears lengthwise; core and cut the quarters crosswise into ⅓-inch-thick slices. Melt the butter in a large skillet over high heat. Add the pear slices, sprinkle with a little salt and toss to coat the slices with the butter. Cook, tossing often, for 5 minutes, or until they are softened but still hold their shape. Add the zest and pepper and toss to coat well.

Transfer to a bowl, squeeze with lemon juice and toss. Alternatively, serve the sautéed pears with lemon wedges on the side.

Variations

* Add ground fennel seeds or aniseeds to taste (start with ¼ teaspoon) with the zest and pepper.

* Add a handful of fresh or dried cranberries to the butter and the pears.

* Sauté some sliced onions in the butter before you add the pears. Add a splash or two of raspberry vinegar with the lemon juice.

Orange *and* Red Pepper Compote

Serves 6

THE SWEETNESS of this chunky relish comes from red peppers, oranges and basil. They are balanced by shallots and white wine. Serve at room temperature (or in the hot summer months, chilled) with fish, particularly salmon or swordfish, as well as with other seafood, poultry, pork, duck or game.

1   cup orange juice

1   cup dry white wine

2   tablespoons balsamic or white
    wine vinegar

6   shallots, coarsely chopped
    A few basil stems, plus ¼ cup
      chopped fresh basil

4   navel oranges

2   large sweet red peppers

2   tablespoons olive oil
    Salt
    Freshly ground black pepper

Place the orange juice, wine, vinegar, shallots and basil stems in a small nonreactive saucepan. Remove 2 strips of orange zest, each about 3 inches long, from the oranges with a vegetable peeler and add to the saucepan. Bring to a boil over high heat, reduce the heat to medium and simmer until the liquid has been reduced to 1 cup, about 15 minutes.

While the sauce reduces, peel the oranges, removing all the white pith. Cut the oranges into ¼-inch-thick slices and arrange on a deep plate or in a wide bowl. Scatter the chopped basil over the oranges. When the sauce has reduced, strain it over the oranges and basil. Set the compote aside.

Core, seed and quarter the peppers. Cut each quarter crosswise into ½-inch-wide strips. Heat the oil in a medium skillet over medium-high heat and add the peppers. Season with salt and pepper and toss well. Cook the peppers for 5 minutes, stirring frequently, until slightly softened, then add to the orange-basil compote. Gently stir to combine the mixture. The orange slices will break up; that is fine. Let the compote cool to room temperature and serve. The compote may also be served chilled.

Sweet-*and*-Sour Stuffed Apples

Serves 4

HALVED APPLES ARE FILLED with a mixture reminiscent of turkey stuffing—bread crumbs, onion, herbs and chopped apple—with vinegar and raisins imparting an Italian sweet-and-sour flavor. The baked apples make a nice addition to a holiday meal and work well on a buffet.

2   large tart green apples, such as
    Granny Smith
1   tablespoon unsalted butter
1   small onion, chopped
¾   teaspoon each freshly chopped thyme
    and marjoram or ¼ teaspoon each
    dried (or try sage, savory or rosemary)
    Salt
    Freshly ground black pepper
2   tablespoons dark raisins
2   tablespoons cider vinegar
¼   cup fresh bread crumbs

Preheat the oven to 350 degrees F.

Cut the apples in half crosswise and core. Scoop out the apples, leaving a ⅓-to-½-inch border. Chop the apple you have scooped out; set aside.

Melt the butter in a medium skillet over medium heat. Add the onion, herbs, ¼ teaspoon salt and some pepper and cook for about 5 minutes to brown the onion. Add the raisins and vinegar and cook 1 minute more, or until the vinegar mostly evaporates. Add the reserved chopped apple to the mixture, along with the bread crumbs, and mix well.

Season the apple cavities with salt and pepper and fill with the stuffing. Transfer the apples to a 9-inch cake pan, cover and bake for 40 to 45 minutes, or until the apples have softened. Uncover, raise the heat to 400 degrees F and bake 10 minutes more, or until the tops are browned and the apples are tender when pierced with the tip of a knife. Serve hot from the oven, or let them sit and serve warm; they will be equally delicious either way.

Variations

* Top the stuffed apples with chopped walnuts or grated Parmesan cheese or a mixture of the two.

* Add crisped bacon, crumbled, to the stuffing along with some chopped scallion.

* Replace the herbs with chopped watercress and top the apples with chopped walnuts.

* Replace the onion with 1 medium leek and the raisins with dried cranberries.

Oranges *and* Ginger

Serves 4 to 6

THIS DISH COULDN'T BE SIMPLER. The orange slices are sprinkled with sweet spices, brown sugar and orange zest. Chilling is all that's left to do, and the sugar draws out the juices to form a syrupy sauce.

This recipe was inspired by a dish in Nina Simonds's *China Express* (William Morrow, 1993). Serve with seafood, especially salmon, as well as poultry, duck, pork, lamb or beef.

> 6 **navel oranges**
> 2 **tablespoons light brown sugar**
> 1 **tablespoon (tightly packed)**
>   **minced crystallized ginger**
> 1 **teaspoon ground cinnamon**
>   **Mint sprigs (optional)**

Using a vegetable peeler or a sharp knife, remove 4 strips of orange zest from 1 orange, trying not to remove any of the bitter white pith. Cut the zest into angel-hair-thin strips on an angle. Bring a small pot of water to a boil. Add the zest and blanch for 1 minute. Drain and rinse under cold water. Dry and set aside, covered with plastic.

Using a large knife, remove all the skin and white pith from the 6 oranges. To do this, cut a slice from the end of each orange. Stand the orange on end on a cutting board. Using long sawing motions, cut off the peel at the surface of the flesh, cutting from top to bottom. Continue until all peel has been removed. Turn the orange upside down and trim any remaining peel and pith, then turn the orange on its side and cut crosswise into ¼-inch-thick slices. Repeat with the remaining oranges. Arrange the slices in an overlapping pattern on a large platter.

In a small bowl, mix the brown sugar, crystallized ginger and cinnamon. Sprinkle the mixture on the oranges and sprinkle with the reserved orange zest. Cover and let sit at room temperature to blend the flavors, at least ½ hour. If you want to serve the oranges cold, let marinate, covered, in the refrigerator. Decorate with mint sprigs, if desired, and serve.

Variations

* Add ¼ to ½ teaspoon vanilla to the brown-sugar mixture. Sprinkle the mixture over the oranges.

* Sprinkle minced basil or chervil over the dish before decorating it with the mint.

* Mix ½ to 1 teaspoon dry English mustard into the brown-sugar mixture and sprinkle over the oranges.

* Make this dish with melon, such as cantaloupe, crenshaw, honeydew or a mixture of melons.

Chapter Two

Cold Vegetable Dishes

MY GRANDFATHER had the right idea. On hot summer nights, I often think of him on the porch in his big-city-lawyer weekend clothes, poised over a bowl of icy cucumber slices that were sprinkled with sugar and mint and floated like lily pads in a pool of apple cider vinegar. On those evenings, supper usually would be a cookout. Staples were hamburgers, hot dogs, chicken and, of course, the cucumbers. Satisfied with his choice of relief from the sweltering August, Gramp would cap his dinner with a huge glass of buttermilk.

While there is nothing more refreshing on a hot day, cold vegetable dishes are welcome in all seasons, not only when the weather is thick with humidity. Their temperature complements a meal in a way that no other dish can. In chilly months, they bring a reviving note of contrast to a hot meal; in the warmer months, they cool and restore. And for sure, when I find a cold dish on my plate, I sit up and pay attention.

That's one of the principal advantages of chilling rather than heating vegetables: It introduces the element of surprise. Serving ratatouille—the famous Provençal stew of eggplants, zucchini and tomatoes—cold not only breaks routine but also changes the nature of the dish. The vegetables retain their natural crispness rather than softening completely, and they seem to taste brighter as well.

This is especially true of salads, which are in their natural element chilled. Celery, steamed lightly so it keeps its crunchiness, appreciates in flavor when marinated in a lemony vinaigrette accented with pungent capers and garlic. Tart green apples and lime juice give a traditional slaw made with red cabbage an energetic boost, and

a dashing curry dressing and uncooked shallot slivers set off a mild and creamy avocado salad. As for Gramp's favorite cucumbers—really a sort of instant pickle—I have updated them by adding fresh basil and lemongrass.

Many other side dishes benefit from a stay in the refrigerator. A brief pass over the steaming pot is all peas need before cooling; they remain sweet and smooth, not starchy or olive-drab. Asparagus is easily overcooked, but steaming and chilling ensures its freshness and beauty.

Refrigerating marries the flavors and rounds out the rough edges of ingredients such as feta and vinegar. Steamed zucchini stuffed with a briny mixture of feta cheese, lemon and oregano is good hot, but even more memorable cold. Hot pickled beets taste flatly acidic and lack sweetness. Chilled, the flavors achieve a perfect balance.

REMEMBER THAT SEASONINGS are often muted by cooling: This is no time for faint-heartedness. Add salt, pepper, sugar, vinegars, citrus zest and juices, herbs or spices to wake up flavors that have been quieted by the cold.

All of the recipes in this chapter—from

marinated vegetables to salads to cold stews—go well with both hot and cold meals. Like Gramp's crisp cucumbers, they are particularly complementary with grilled and picnic foods or vegetarian feasts, but they can just as well round out a buffet or holiday table, helping you keep your cool as you prepare for the onslaught of guests.

COLD VEGETABLE DISHES

Three Peas *with* Asian Seasonings

Serves 6

I LIKE THE COOL, bright green shade of these marinated vegetables, the different shapes of the snow, sugar snap and baby peas and the way they glisten when coated with the dressing. Serve with fish, particularly swordfish and bluefish, or with pork loin, pork tenderloin or poultry.

½ **pound snow peas, trimmed**

½ **pound sugar snap peas, trimmed**

2 **pounds fresh peas or 1 cup baby frozen peas (about 5 ounces), thawed**

2 **tablespoons fresh lemon juice**

2 **teaspoons sugar**

1-2 **teaspoons chili paste with garlic**
  Salt

3 **tablespoons dark sesame oil**

2 **tablespoons olive oil**

Place the snow peas in a steamer basket, cover and steam for 2 minutes, or until crisp-tender. Steam the sugar snap peas for 3 minutes, or until crisp-tender. Rinse the snow peas and snap peas under cold water to stop the cooking. Drain, dry and set aside. If using fresh peas, blanch in boiling water in a small saucepan for 2 to 3 minutes, depending on size. Drain, rinse under cold water, drain again and dry. Mix with the other peas in a medium bowl and set aside. If using frozen peas, simply thaw and mix with the other peas.

Make a dressing by mixing the lemon juice, sugar, 1 teaspoon chili paste and ½ teaspoon salt in a small bowl. Slowly whisk in the sesame and olive oils. Taste for seasonings and add more chili paste to make the dressing as spicy as you like. Pour over the peas and toss to coat evenly.

Marinate for at least 1 hour (you can marinate for a short time at room temperature, unless it is a sweltering day) or overnight in the refrigerator; the dish will only improve. Before serving, toss the peas and taste for seasonings; correct if necessary, then serve.

Variations

* Add minced scallions to the dressing and add sliced cucumbers, cut into half-moons, to the peas.

* Add soy sauce, minced fresh ginger and chopped garlic, alone or in combination, to the dressing.

* If you would like another color in the dish, add sliced red peppers or carrots cut into julienne strips.

* Serve this dish with the curry dressing on page 52 in place of the sesame dressing.

Asparagus *with* Gremolata Dressing

Serves 6

GREMOLATA (also spelled gremolada)—a mixture of garlic, parsley and grated lemon zest—is the traditional garnish for the northern Italian braised veal shank dish known as *osso buco*. I have incorporated this lively combination into a citrus vinaigrette for a chilled salad of lightly steamed asparagus. Experiment with the flavors in the gremolata, as Italians do, with such other ingredients as minced anchovies, grated orange zest, chopped rosemary or sage. Serve with braised veal dishes, roast lamb, ham, chicken or fish.

2 tablespoons minced fresh parsley

2 garlic cloves, minced

1 teaspoon (packed) grated lemon zest
   Salt

2 tablespoons fresh lemon juice

1 tablespoon fresh orange juice

6 tablespoons extra-virgin olive oil
   Freshly ground black pepper

2 pounds asparagus, trimmed and rinsed

Place the parsley, garlic, lemon zest, ¼ teaspoon salt, lemon juice and orange juice in a small bowl. Mix with a whisk. Slowly whisk in the oil and season with pepper. Set aside to allow the flavors to blend.

Place the asparagus in a steamer basket and steam for 3 to 5 minutes, depending on the size, or until the spears are tender yet offer a bit of resistance when pierced with the tip of a sharp knife. Transfer to a platter. Give the dressing a final whisk, correct the seasonings with more salt and pepper as needed, and pour over the asparagus. Roll the asparagus in the dressing to coat completely.

Let the asparagus cool to room temperature for about ½ hour, gently rolling the spears in the dressing from time to time. Chill before serving.

Variations

* Add 1 teaspoon (packed) grated orange zest to the dressing along with the lemon zest.

* Add 1 or 2 minced anchovies to the dressing.

* Replace the asparagus with fiddleheads.

Gramp's Cucumbers

Serves 6

To My Grandfather's favorite ice-cold sliced cucumbers with sugar, mint and apple cider vinegar, I've added minced lemongrass and basil, giving the dish an Asian flair. Serve with barbecued chicken, hamburgers, seafood, pork or pasta.

½ cup cider vinegar

¼ cup water

2 tablespoons minced fresh lemongrass
    (1-2 stalks), outer leaves and top half
    of stalks trimmed

2 tablespoons chopped fresh basil
    or 2 teaspoons dried

1 tablespoon chopped fresh mint
    or 1 teaspoon dried

4 teaspoons sugar

   Salt

   Freshly ground black pepper

1½ pounds cucumbers, peeled

Mix all the ingredients, except the cucumbers, in a small bowl, using ½ teaspoon salt and some pepper to taste; set aside.

Slice the cucumbers and arrange half of them in a dish with sides, such as a quiche pan or other pie plate. Sprinkle with additional salt and pepper, whisk the sauce and spoon half of it over the slices. Arrange the remaining cucumbers on top of the sauce and spoon the remaining sauce over the cucumbers.

Cover, refrigerate and marinate for 1 to 2 hours. Serve chilled.

Variations

* Sprinkle the cucumbers with cayenne or red pepper flakes when you add the salt and pepper.

* Use ¾ cup lime juice in place of the vinegar and water.

Cold Stuffed Zucchini

Serves 6

THE FLAVORS OF GREECE combine in this salad. Chopped cooked zucchini, feta cheese, oregano, lemon juice and olive oil are stuffed into lightly steamed zucchini halves. The zucchini are then chilled. Serve in the summer with cold chicken, turkey, seafood or with rice salad and a platter of sliced tomatoes.

Do not skimp on the amount of feta, for its strong bite is essential to the final taste.

3 small zucchini, scrubbed, trimmed, split in half lengthwise

⅓ cup extra-virgin olive oil

4-5 tablespoons fresh lemon juice

8 ounces feta cheese, coarsely crumbled

2 tablespoons chopped fresh parsley

½ tablespoon fresh oregano or 1½ teaspoons dried

Plenty of freshly ground black pepper

6 lettuce leaves

Small cherry tomatoes for garnish (optional)

Black olives for garnish (optional)

Diced red onion for garnish (optional)

Steam the zucchini until tender, 5 to 10 minutes depending on size. Set aside on a plate to cool.

When cool enough to handle, scoop out the zucchini to form boats. Set aside and chop the scooped-out zucchini. Place the chopped zucchini in a bowl and add the oil, 4 tablespoons lemon juice, feta, parsley, oregano and black pepper. Mix well with a fork, breaking up the cheese. Taste and add the remaining 1 tablespoon lemon juice, if desired.

Stuff the zucchini boats with the mixture and place them on a bed of lettuce on a plate or a platter. Cover and chill for 2 to 4 hours.

Serve with the cherry tomatoes, black olives and red onions arranged around the zucchini as garnish, if desired.

Variations

* Use this stuffing to fill avocados or cherry tomatoes. You can also stuff all three (zucchini, avocados and cherry tomatoes) and serve together on a platter.

* Mix diced cucumbers, garlic and dill into the stuffing; omit the oregano.

Pickled Beets

Makes about 1 quart

IN THIS CONDIMENT, the natural sweetness of cooked beets is highlighted by the delicate acidity of raspberry vinegar and by sweet onion. When selecting the vinegar, check the label for the percentage of acidity (listed as either acetic acid or acidity), and make sure that it is no more than 5 percent. Any higher and the finished dish will be too harsh, the raspberry flavor obliterated.

1 bunch beets (about 1½ pounds without greens), approximately 4 beets
1½ cups raspberry vinegar (4.5-5% acidity)
3 tablespoons sugar
Salt
1 large garlic clove, crushed
12 whole peppercorns
1 bay leaf
1 sweet onion, such as Vidalia or Maui (8-10 ounces), cut into ¼-inch-thick slices

Place the beets in a medium saucepan, cover with water and boil until tender, 45 to 60 minutes. Alternatively, place them in a steamer basket over water, cover and steam, checking the water level occasionally and replenishing if necessary. Transfer to a plate to cool.

Meanwhile, combine the vinegar, sugar, ½ teaspoon salt, garlic, peppercorns and bay leaf in a small nonreactive saucepan. Bring to a boil and boil 5 minutes. Remove from the heat and set aside to cool. Remove the bay leaf.

When the beets are cool enough to handle, peel, cut into wedges and place in a large bowl. Add the vinegar mixture and onion slices and toss together well. Cover, refrigerate and let marinate for a minimum of 24 hours. Serve chilled.

Chilled Ratatouille

Serves 6 to 8

RATATOUILLE, a light Provençal medley of eggplant, onions, garlic, sweet peppers, zucchini and tomatoes, is usually served hot or at room temperature. For a refreshing change, I like it chilled with a squeeze of lemon juice and a scattering of black olive slivers. Enjoy with scrambled eggs or omelettes for breakfast or brunch, or for dinner with grilled or roasted meats, poultry or seafood.

½ cup olive oil

1 pound eggplant, peeled and
   cut into ½-inch dice
   Salt
   Freshly ground black pepper

1 pound onions (about 3 medium),
   sliced ¼-½ inch thick

½ pound sweet peppers, red, orange
   or yellow, cut into ½-inch dice

4 large garlic cloves, minced

1 pound zucchini, cut into ½-inch dice

1 pound tomatoes (about 3 medium),
   cored and cut into 1-inch pieces

1 bay leaf

1 tablespoon fresh thyme leaves
   or 1 teaspoon dried
   Cayenne pepper

2-8 tablespoons fresh lemon juice, to taste
   Lemon wedges

½ cup black olives, pitted and sliced

Heat ¼ cup of the oil in a large nonreactive skillet or Dutch oven over medium heat. Add the eggplant, season with ¼ teaspoon salt and some pepper, and cook for 7 minutes, or until softened, tossing often. Remove to a bowl.

Reduce the heat to medium-low and add the remaining ¼ cup oil to the skillet. Add the onions, sprinkle with ¼ teaspoon salt and some pepper, stir, cover and sauté for about 20 minutes, uncovering to stir often, until the onions are soft with very little color. Uncover and add the peppers and garlic.

Sprinkle with ¼ teaspoon salt and some pepper, stir, cover and cook for 10 minutes more, uncovering occasionally to stir. Add the zucchini, season with ¼ teaspoon salt and some pepper, stir, cover and cook another 5 minutes, stirring often. Uncover the skillet and add the tomatoes, bay leaf, thyme, cayenne to taste and the reserved eggplant. Stew for 1 hour, with the cover askew, stirring often.

When done, transfer the ratatouille to a bowl and cool to room temperature, then refrigerate to chill. To serve, remove the bay leaf and correct the seasonings, adding more salt, pepper and cayenne if needed, and squeeze with as much lemon juice as you want. Serve in bowls garnished with lemon wedges and scattered with the black olive slices.

Variation

*To serve this dish hot, omit the lemon juice and wedges and the black olives.

Grilled Caponata

Serves 6

Caponata is a sweet-and-sour Italian eggplant salad. Traditionally, the vegetables are sautéed, but here they are grilled for a smoky taste. Currants or raisins contribute sweetness. This salad is a delicious summer accompaniment to any grilled meat, poultry, fish or shellfish and may be served either chilled or at room temperature. It is also wonderful with a baked potato or main-course pasta dish for a vegetarian meal.

Olive oil for brushing vegetables

1 large onion, Spanish, red or Vidalia, sliced ⅓ inch thick

2 medium eggplants, sliced lengthwise ⅓ inch thick

4 large celery stalks, trimmed

1 large ripe tomato, cut into ⅓-inch dice

Salt

Freshly ground black pepper

About ½ cup balsamic or red wine vinegar

½ cup pitted green olives

¼ cup drained capers, rinsed and drained again

¼ cup dried currants or dark raisins

¼ cup chopped fresh parsley

2 tablespoons pine nuts, toasted (optional); see page 22

Prepare the grill by lighting the coals.

Brush the onion, eggplant and celery on both sides with the olive oil. When the coals are ready (there should be no flames, just glowing red coals with a layer of gray ash around them), grill the vegetables, 6 to 8 inches from the coals, until browned. The onion will take 5 to 7 minutes per side; it should remain slightly crunchy. The eggplant will take 2 to 3 minutes per side and should be soft. The celery will take 2 to 3 minutes per side; it should remain slightly crunchy.

Have a cutting board ready and, as the vegetables cook, remove them from the grill and cut crosswise into ⅓-inch-thick slices. Transfer them to a platter or large bowl.

Add the tomato to the grilled vegetables, season with 1 teaspoon salt and some pepper and toss well. Add the vinegar and toss. Add the remaining ingredients, except the nuts, and stir to combine.

Cool to room temperature and refrigerate for at least 4 hours, preferably overnight, to let the flavors blend. Taste and correct the seasonings, adding more vinegar, salt and pepper if needed.

If you would like, let the salad return to room temperature before serving. Sprinkle with the nuts and serve.

Variations

* Quarter, stem and seed 1 large sweet red pepper and brush it with oil; grill skin side down until evenly blackened, peel the pepper quarters, cut into ⅓-inch dice and add to the grilled vegetables. Trim 1 zucchini, slice lengthwise, brush with oil, grill, cut into ⅓-inch dice and add to the vegetables.

* Add 2 garlic cloves, minced, along with the vinegar and remaining ingredients.

Red Cabbage *and* Green Apple Salad

Serves 8

LIME AND MINT give refreshing overtones to a crisp salad of cabbage and apples. If you would like to serve the salad on a platter, pile it on a bed of spinach. This dish improves as it sits; don't be afraid to marinate it overnight.

¼ cup fresh lime juice

2 tablespoons fresh lemon juice

1 bunch scallions (6-8), green parts only, cut into 2-inch pieces

½ cup (packed) fresh mint leaves

2 garlic cloves, quartered

1 teaspoon sugar

Salt

¾ cup extra-virgin olive oil

Freshly ground black pepper

1 small red cabbage (1¼-1½ pounds)

3 large green apples (1¼-1½ pounds)

Place the lime and lemon juice, scallion greens, mint, garlic, sugar and ½ teaspoon salt in a blender. Puree until smooth. With the machine on low, add the oil in a steady stream. Add some pepper and set aside while you make the slaw.

Trim, quarter and core the red cabbage. Cut the quarters into thin slices crosswise and transfer to a medium bowl. Quarter the apples lengthwise, core and peel. Cut the apples into thin slices crosswise and add to the bowl.

Whisk the dressing, taste, and correct the seasonings, adding more salt and pepper if needed. Pour the dressing over the salad.

Toss the salad. Let marinate at least 1 hour or overnight in the refrigerator, tossing occasionally. Serve chilled.

Variations

* You can add ¼ pound red onion (about ½ of a large one), cut into thin slivers.

* For a more classic slaw, make this with green cabbage and add some shredded carrots along with the apples.

* Make the dressing with all lemon juice and substitute walnut oil for half of the olive oil. Use ordinary olive oil with this version, not extra-virgin.

Celery Salad *with* Capers *and* Dill

Serves 6

THIS CRUNCHY SALAD of steamed celery is marinated and chilled in a lemon-olive oil dressing spiked with capers, garlic and dill. When I brought this Shaker dish to a pot-luck dinner one night, everyone loved it. Serve with eggplant Parmesan or lasagna for a vegetarian meal, or with chicken, seafood or pork.

1 tablespoon fresh lemon juice

1 large garlic clove or 2 medium, minced

Salt

Freshly ground black pepper

2 tablespoons extra-virgin olive oil

2 tablespoons chopped fresh dill

2 tablespoons drained capers, rinsed and drained again

2 pounds celery

Place the lemon juice, garlic, ⅛ teaspoon salt and some pepper in a small bowl. Whisk to dissolve the salt. Add the oil in a stream, whisking until homogenous. Stir in the dill and capers and set aside to let the flavors develop.

Wash and trim the celery stalks. Cut into ½-inch slices on an angle. Place in a steamer basket and steam for 5 to 7 minutes, or until the celery is tender yet retains some crispness. Transfer to a bowl. Correct the seasonings of the dressing, adding more salt and pepper if needed. Pour the dressing over the celery. Mix thoroughly and let cool to room temperature.

Cover and refrigerate until chilled, tossing occasionally, and marinate 1 to 2 hours. Serve chilled.

Variations

* Instead of the dill, add any herb that you like: parsley, tarragon, chives or chervil, alone or in combination. All four together constitute the classic French herb combination called *fines herbes*.

* Use apple cider vinegar and vegetable oil, such as safflower, corn or canola, in place of the lemon juice and olive oil.

Avocado Curry

Serves 4

SOFT AVOCADOS in this cold salad are nicely set off by crunchy bits of shallots and carrot shavings and topped with a curry dressing. The curry must be gently heated in a bit of the oil to remove the raw starchy taste of the turmeric. Serve this beautiful salad with roasted meats, poultry, seafood or with a crisp loaf of bread for lunch or a light supper.

For the curry dressing

4 tablespoons olive oil

1 teaspoon curry powder

2 tablespoons fresh lime juice

1 tablespoon fresh lemon juice

Salt

Freshly ground black pepper (optional)

2 avocados, soft and ripe, peeled and cut lengthwise into ¼-inch-thick slices

1 large shallot (1-2 ounces), peeled and sliced paper thin

1 large carrot, peeled and shredded

To make the curry dressing: Heat 1 tablespoon of the oil in a small skillet. Remove from the heat, add the curry powder and swirl in the oil to heat it. Transfer to a small bowl. Add the citrus juices and ¼ teaspoon salt; whisk to combine. Pour in the remaining 3 tablespoons oil, whisking continuously. Taste and add more salt and pepper, if needed.

Arrange the avocado slices on a large plate. Scatter the shallots and carrot over the avocado. Pour the dressing over and serve immediately, or let the dish marinate for about 30 minutes in the refrigerator before serving.

Chapter Three

Hot Vegetable Dishes

IN EARLY SPRING, I look forward to the arrival of tightly wound fiddleheads—immature forms of ostrich ferns—which poke up from the marshes long before peas, spinach or other greens have appeared in the garden. So called because they resemble the scrolls of fiddles, fiddleheads are harvested before they unravel to a full, sweeping green. In flavor, they are similar to asparagus but less sweet, and their texture is suggestive of broccoli. For the few brief weeks they are available, I enjoy them almost daily.

ONE OF MY FAVORITE PREPARATIONS for them is the simplest. Knowing that, in France, asparagus is often eaten with butter that is cooked to a deep, nut-flavored brown, I decided to apply the technique to fiddleheads, drizzling the butter over their curlicues, then dusting them with Parmesan cheese. The resulting Brown-Butter Fiddleheads have become something of an annual specialty in my kitchen.

Unlike most produce, which, whatever the quality, is now available year-round, fiddleheads are one of the few remaining genuinely seasonal pleasures. They remind us that fresh, local vegetables always taste better than out-of-season ones and are cheaper, too.

Radishes, another eagerly awaited bonus of spring, are more common than fiddleheads and become a new sensation when sautéed quickly in butter. Prepared that way, Creamed Radishes retain their peppery crunch and are finished with a coating of smooth, sweet cream. In late spring, sweet onions, such as Vidalia or Maui, are now widely available in many supermarkets. In Onion and Berry Melt, their sweetness is heightened by caramelizing them in butter and combining them with the sting of raspberry vinegar and the richness of black currant jam.

As surely as fiddleheads, the first radishes and sweet onions mean spring, corn on the cob is the highlight of summer. I like it in two simple preparations. I simmer it in heavy cream, seasoning it with a touch of sage. Alternatively, I sauté it with scallion slivers and plenty of black pepper. To take advantage of the succession of crops in the garden, I often make up a skillet of Vegetable Jardinière, mixing freshly picked, thin green beans, green and yellow summer squash, sweet peppers of all colors and a handful of cherry tomatoes with plenty of chopped fresh herbs.

The harvest of late-season orange squashes in the fall presents an occasion for celebration in my kitchen. Braised Garlic and Buttercup Squash combines softly cooked, chunky squash and whole garlic cloves. The squash partially falls apart, and the garlic melts in your mouth. In Winter Squash Parmesan, a hearty side dish that doubles for eggplant Parmesan, slices of butternut or buttercup squash alternate with cheese and tomato sauce.

IN THE WINTER, a lean time for vegetables where I live, I like to play around with old favorites. To update braised red cabbage, I add dried pears rather than the usual apples for a more concentrated flavor. I braise cauliflower with browned butter instead of smothering it in cheese sauce. To startle carrots out of their winter anonymity, I toss in a handful of sautéed garlic cloves and a dusting of fresh herbs.

Roasting is to winter what grilling is to summer, offering endless variations and ease in cooking, since the foolproof technique requires nothing more than a high-heat oven. Possibilities range from carrots, onions and potatoes scattered around a Sunday roast to fresh ideas like leeks and potatoes, or baby beets and whole garlic cloves, or fennel wedges served alone or with potatoes.

If anything, my side dishes are apt to be even more inventive in winter than when fresh produce is more plentiful. Encompassing a range of styles, they represent the triumph of ingenuity over the natural limits of the season.

Hot Vegetable Dishes

Creamed Radishes

Serves 4 to 6

SERVED AS A HOT VEGETABLE, radishes remain crisp and peppery and add color to the dinner plate. The vinegar in this recipe helps set the color. Serve with grilled steaks or fish.

- 2 bunches radishes
- 1 tablespoon unsalted butter
- 1 tablespoon sherry vinegar
- Salt
- Freshly ground black pepper
- ½ cup heavy cream
- 1 tablespoon snipped fresh chives

Wash and trim the radishes; cut them into wedges.

Melt the butter in a large nonreactive skillet over high heat. Add the radish wedges and toss to coat. Add the vinegar, ¼ teaspoon salt and some pepper and cook 5 minutes, or until translucent, stirring often. Add the cream and reduce it over high heat until it coats the radishes, 2 to 3 minutes.

Transfer the radishes and sauce to a serving bowl and stir in the chives. Serve immediately.

Variation

* Omit the cream for a light version.

Brown-Butter Fiddleheads

Serves 4

THIS DISH IS A TESTAMENT to the adage "The simpler, the better." Fiddleheads are tightly rolled-up fern shoots that are harvested in early spring. They have a very short season but are now available in some supermarkets. Fiddleheads are reminiscent of asparagus but are less sweet. Browned butter, known as *noisette* butter in France, complements them with its nutty, rich taste. The flavor of the dish depends on the butter, so make sure it is brown, not pale golden. Serve with everything!

1 **pound fiddleheads**
2 **tablespoons unsalted butter**
  Salt
  Freshly ground black pepper
2-3 **tablespoons freshly grated**
   Parmesan cheese

Wash the fiddleheads and remove the brown paper-like covering; rinse again. Place them in a steamer basket, cover and steam 3 to 5 minutes, or until crisp-tender, depending on their size.

While the fiddleheads steam, place the butter in a small skillet and cook over medium-high heat, swirling the skillet frequently, until well browned.

When the fiddleheads are done, transfer to a serving bowl and pour the butter over them. Sprinkle with salt and pepper to taste and toss to coat the fiddleheads. Sprinkle them with the cheese and serve.

Variations

* Substitute asparagus for the fiddleheads for an equally delicious dish.

* Try this butter with fresh peas in place of the fiddleheads and scatter crisped and crumbled pancetta on top.

Wilted Greens

Serves 4

A CLASSIC DISH IN MANY CULTURES, greens that are gently steamed until just wilted are nutritious and quick to prepare. Do not soak the greens in water, for that will bring out their natural bitterness. Instead, rinse them quickly under running cold water and shake off the excess. There is no need to dry the greens; the water clinging to their leaves aids the steaming process. Serve with chicken, baked pasta or my favorite partner for this dish, spaghetti and meatballs.

1 large head escarole, 1 pound spinach
    or 1 large bunch Swiss chard
2 tablespoons extra-virgin olive oil
    or flavored olive oil, such as
    hot pepper, garlic or herb
2 garlic cloves, minced
    Salt
    Freshly ground black pepper
    Freshly ground nutmeg

Wash the greens and remove the stems, if they are tough. Shake out excess water and tear into large pieces. Leave some water clinging to the leaves.

Heat the oil in a large, deep pot over medium heat. Add the garlic and cook, stirring, for 30 seconds. Add the greens and toss them in the oil. Cover and cook until the greens start to wilt, 1 to 3 minutes depending on the type of greens.

Uncover, toss the greens, cover again and continue to cook until completely wilted, 3 to 5 minutes for spinach, 5 minutes for chard and 5 to 7 minutes for escarole. When the greens are done, uncover, season with salt, pepper and nutmeg and serve.

Variations

* Vary the greens, using mustard, turnip, beet, dandelion, kale, collard or chicory.

* Sprinkle Parmesan cheese over the greens just before serving.

* Wilt the greens with raisins and top the dish with toasted pine nuts (see page 22).

* Sauté some chopped green apple in the oil. Add the garlic and continue with the recipe.

* Add minced anchovy with the garlic and scatter chopped green olives and capers over the finished dish.

Vegetable Jardinière

Serves 6

JARDINIÈRE is a mixture of vegetables of any kind. This combination features carrots, summer squashes, radishes, peas and cucumbers. You can use any vegetables you prefer, and I have given other suggestions. The flavored butter coating the jardinière, known as a compound butter, is a blend of garlic, herbs, grated lemon zest and softened butter. It, too, can be experimented with. Freeze any extra butter that you do not use; it keeps for several months.

5   tablespoons unsalted butter, softened
1   garlic clove, minced
1   tablespoon chopped fresh chives, mint, dill, parsley or scallion tops or 1 teaspoon dried herb of choice
1   teaspoon grated lemon zest
    Salt
    Freshly ground black pepper
2   medium carrots
1   small or medium zucchini
1   small or medium yellow summer squash
1   bunch radishes
½   pound snow peas or sugar snap peas
½   long seedless European cucumber

In a small bowl, combine 4 tablespoons of the butter with the garlic, herb of choice, lemon zest, ¼ teaspoon salt and some pepper. Mix with a fork until smooth. Taste for seasonings and set aside.

Peel the carrots, cut in half lengthwise and cut into half-moon slices on an angle. Trim the ends off the squashes, cut in half lengthwise and cut into half-moon slices on an angle. Trim ends off the radishes and slice. String the snow or sugar snap peas. Peel the cucumber, cut in half lengthwise and cut into half-moon slices on an angle.

Melt the remaining 1 tablespoon butter in a large skillet over medium heat. Add the carrots, toss with the butter, add a few drops of water, cover and cook for 5 minutes. Uncover, add the squashes and radishes and toss well. Cook, uncovered, for 5 minutes more, or until the squashes and radishes soften. Add the peas and cucumber, toss and cook 5 minutes more, or until crisp-tender. Season with ¼ teaspoon salt and some pepper and remove from the heat.

Add as much of the flavored butter as you like and toss to coat the vegetables. Serve immediately.

Variations

* Try substituting an equal amount of any of the following for any one of the vegetables in the recipe: cauliflower, broccoli, purple-topped turnips, red peppers, green beans, fennel, ordinary peas or celery.

* Make a different butter. Instead of this one, try one with curry; or chopped roasted red pepper, lemon zest and chopped black olives; or toasted nuts (see page 22) and scallions.

Onion *and* Berry Melt

Serves 6

REMINISCENT OF MARMALADE, this is a melt-in-your-mouth combination of slowly browned onions, raspberry vinegar and black currant jam. Give the onions all the time they need to cook; there should be no remaining crunch. Serve with chicken, roast turkey breast, turkey burgers, ham, sausages, pork, hamburgers or fish.

4 tablespoons unsalted butter

2 pounds sweet onions, such as
  Vidalia or Maui, sliced ¼ inch thick
  Salt
  Freshly ground black pepper

2 tablespoons raspberry vinegar

½ cup black currant jam

Melt the butter in a large nonreactive skillet over medium heat. Add the onions, ½ teaspoon salt and some pepper; toss to coat the onions. Cover and cook for about 10 minutes, stirring occasionally, until the onions lose their moisture.

Uncover and cook for 30 to 45 minutes more, or until the onions are brown and soft. Add the vinegar and black currant jam and cook for 5 minutes more to melt the jam. Correct the seasonings, adding more salt and pepper if needed, and serve.

Variations

* Add 2 tablespoons cassis (black currant liqueur) just before serving.

* Add chopped fresh chives, mint, thyme, tarragon or chervil just before serving.

Creamed Corn

Serves 4

THIS OLD-FASHIONED GEM is simple to make and far superior in taste and texture to anything packaged. The corn is scraped from the cob, producing lots of sweet milk. To make the dish even more luxuriant, the kernels are cooked with heavy cream. Enjoy with roast chicken and ripe tomato slices.

4 large ears sweet corn, husks
    and silks removed
1 cup heavy or whipping cream
2 tablespoons chopped fresh sage
    or 2 teaspoons dried (optional)
Salt
Freshly ground black pepper

Using a sharp knife, make closely spaced parallel slits down each row of kernels, slicing through the center of each kernel. Using the back of the knife, scrape the corn into a bowl to remove all the kernels and milk. You should end up with 2 to 3 cups corn and milk.

Transfer to a medium saucepan and add the cream and sage, if using. Bring to a boil over medium-high heat, reduce the heat to medium and cook until thick and creamy, 20 to 30 minutes. Season with salt and pepper as needed, and serve in small bowls.

Variations

* Add an equal amount of diced or shredded yellow summer squash sautéed in butter and seasoned with salt and pepper.

* To turn this dish into a sauce, add minced garlic and parsley to the finished corn. Spoon it over marinated and grilled boneless chicken breasts.

Sautéed Corn *with* Scallions

Serves 4

MY FATHER'S FAVORITE summer vegetable is steamed corn on the cob. This crisp, spicy, sweet dish is a refreshing change. It is easy to prepare and takes less than 10 minutes, from husking to serving. Serve with turkey breast scallopini, hamburgers, roast chicken or salmon.

4 large ears sweet corn, husks and
   silks removed

2 tablespoons unsalted butter

¾ cup sliced scallions, green parts only

½ teaspoon freshly ground black pepper
   Salt

Using a sharp knife, cut the whole kernels off the cob; you will have 2 to 3 cups.

Melt the butter in a large skillet over high heat and brown it slightly, 1 minute or less. Add the corn, toss to coat it with the butter and cook 3 minutes, tossing often, or until crisp-tender. Add the scallions, and the pepper and salt to taste. Stir well and serve.

"Two Dozen" Carrots

Serves 4

THESE CARROTS ARE COOKED over low heat until they are soft and tender, which brings out their sweetness. The two dozen garlic cloves that are added also become meltingly sweet. If you use oil-cured black olives, the taste of the final dish will be stronger and the color will be striking. Serve with poultry, fish, beef or lamb.

Place the oil in a large skillet over high heat. Add the carrots and garlic; sprinkle with ¼ teaspoon salt. Toss to coat the vegetables with the oil. Cook 1 minute, toss again and cook 1 minute more. If using dried herbs, add them to the carrots now.

Reduce the heat to low, cover and cook for 20 minutes, stirring occasionally, or until the vegetables are soft and tender. Add the olives, toss, cover and cook for 2 minutes more to heat the olives through. Season well with pepper and more salt, if needed. If using a fresh herb, add it now, toss well and serve.

2 tablespoons olive oil

1 pound carrots, peeled and sliced
    ½ inch thick on the diagonal

24 whole garlic cloves, peeled
    (if large, cut in half)
    Salt

1 tablespoon chopped fresh thyme, basil
    or parsley leaves or 1 teaspoon dried
    herb of choice (optional)

24 black olives, oil- or brine-cured, pitted
    Freshly ground black pepper

Roasted Vegetables *and* Variations

Serves 4 to 6

ROASTING VEGETABLES in a hot oven not only caramelizes their outer layers but concentrates their flavors. The result is wonderfully intense. The possibilities are limited only by the availability of ingredients. Roast any vegetable you like, from asparagus to zucchini, with flavorings and seasonings to complement your choice. You can, of course, combine many vegetables into one dish as well.

1 pound carrots, peeled and trimmed

3 medium onions (about 1 pound)

   About 2 tablespoons olive oil

   Salt

   Freshly ground black pepper

Preheat the oven to 400 degrees F.

Cut the carrots into 1-inch chunks on an angle.

Cut the onions into wedges through the root, about 1 inch at the widest part. Place the vegetables in a large bowl and pour on enough oil to coat, starting with about 2 tablespoons. Sprinkle with a healthy dose of salt and pepper and toss until the vegetables are completely coated with oil. Transfer the vegetables to a 13-by-9-inch baking dish.

Roast the vegetables in the oven for 20 minutes. Toss with a metal spatula, scraping up any brown parts and moving everything around. Roast for 20 minutes more and toss again to help the vegetables brown evenly. Roast another 20 minutes more, or until the vegetables are tender when pierced with the tip of a knife; the total cooking time is usually about 1 hour. Serve the roasted vegetables from the baking dish.

Variations

* Add 1 pound parsnips to the above mixture. You will probably need a bit more oil.

* Roast fennel wedges, either by themselves, or mixed with green beans or with little red potatoes. If roasting the fennel alone, mix in a bit of honey and lemon juice for the last 20 minutes of cooking. If roasting them with green beans, mix in chopped fennel greens, or fresh parsley, chervil or tarragon when the beans are done. If roasting them with red potatoes, mix in a little dry mustard diluted with water and some fresh herbs, such as chives, basil, tarragon or oregano, when the potatoes are done.

* Roast asparagus and mix in sliced scallions for the last 20 minutes of cooking.

* Roast baby carrots with peanut oil and dark sesame oil, soy sauce, ground aniseeds or five-spice powder, and serve with lemon wedges.

* Roast whole shallots either by themselves, with mushrooms or with garlic cloves. If roasting shallots by themselves (45 to 60 minutes), you may splash them with balsamic vinegar when done. Or choose a meaty mushroom, such as portobellos, and roast in a separate pan for about 30 minutes. When they are done, mix together the mushrooms and shallots and toss with Dijon mustard and fresh minced thyme. If roasting the shallots with garlic, when the two are done, mix them with fresh herbs, such as thyme, savory, parsley or chives.

* Roast trimmed, cleaned leeks either by themselves or with baby red potatoes. Scatter fresh thyme or tarragon over the finished dish.

* Roast baby beets, cut into halves or wedges, and whole garlic cloves. Finish with a drop of orange juice, if you like.

Braised Red Cabbage *and* Pears

Serves 6 to 8

AN OTHERWISE TRADITIONAL DISH of braised cabbage acquires a touch of sweetness from dried pears in this delicious variation, which is made on the stovetop.

4 tablespoons unsalted butter

1 red onion (8-10 ounces),
    peeled and sliced
    Salt
    Freshly ground black pepper

1 small red cabbage (about 2 pounds),
    trimmed, quartered, cored and
    cut crosswise into ¼-to-½-inch-
    thick slices

4 ounces dried pear halves (8-9), cut
    crosswise into ¼-inch-thick slices

2-3 tablespoons chopped fresh marjoram
    or 1 tablespoon dried

2 tablespoons fresh lemon juice

Melt the butter in a large sauté pan or Dutch oven with a lid over medium heat. Add the onion slices, season with ½ teaspoon salt and some pepper and toss to coat. Sauté the onion, stirring, for about 5 minutes, or until it loses its moisture and softens.

Add the cabbage, pears and marjoram and toss together. Cook, stirring, for 5 minutes to wilt the cabbage. Reduce the heat to low, cover and cook 30 to 45 minutes more, tossing every 5 to 10 minutes, until the cabbage is soft. Stir in the lemon juice, taste and correct the seasonings, adding more salt and pepper if needed, and serve.

Variations

* You can use dried apples in place of the pears.

* If you prefer to braise the dish in the oven, preheat the oven to 325 degrees F. After sautéing the cabbage and pears in a Dutch oven for 5 minutes on the stovetop, cover and place the pot in the oven and bake for 50 to 60 minutes, tossing only once during the cooking.

Brown-Braised Cauliflower

Serves 4

THIS DISH IS SOOTHING and comforting. The key is to cook the cauliflower until it is very soft.

1 cauliflower head (about 2½ pounds)
4 tablespoons unsalted butter
¼ cup water
1 tablespoon chopped fresh rosemary
    or ½-1 teaspoon dried
    Salt
    Freshly ground black pepper

Trim the cauliflower and cut into florets. Cut any large pieces in half. Melt the butter over low heat in a large skillet with a lid. Add the cauliflower and toss to coat with the butter. Cover and let brown, stirring often with a metal spatula, about 5 minutes.

Add the water and rosemary, stir and cover. Cook, stirring occasionally, for 30 to 40 minutes depending on the size of the cauliflower pieces, or until they are tender when pierced with the tip of a knife. There should be very little water left in the pan. Season with salt and pepper and serve.

Variations

* Add garlic to the butter along with the cauliflower and brown the two together. Add crushed hot red pepper along with the rosemary.

* Add raisins with the rosemary and finish the dish with lemon juice and toasted pine nuts (see page 22).

* Finish the dish with coarsely chopped green olives, lemon zest and lemon juice.

* Sauté diced onion in the butter before adding the cauliflower. Add capers at the end of cooking.

* To roast the cauliflower, cut into pieces as directed, then toss in a bowl with 1 tablespoon olive oil, 2 tablespoons melted unsalted butter, and the salt and rosemary. Place in a roasting pan and roast at 400 degrees F for 50 to 60 minutes, tossing every 20 minutes, until the cauliflower is browned and tender. Season with salt and pepper to taste.

Winter Squash Parmesan

Serves 8

SLICES OF ORANGE SQUASH replace the traditional eggplant in this layered oven-baked casserole with tomato sauce and cheese. Whenever I serve it, people are surprised to learn that it is squash, not pasta, for the dish reminds them of lasagna. Serve warm, at room temperature or cold as part of an antipasto.

1 winter squash, butternut or buttercup (2½-3 pounds)

6 cups tomato or spaghetti sauce of choice, preferably homemade

¾ pound Italian fontina cheese, grated

¾ pound mozzarella cheese, grated

1 cup freshly grated Parmesan cheese

Preheat the oven to 350 degrees F.

Cut the squash in half lengthwise, peel and remove the seeds. Cut into thin slices (about ⅛ inch thick) and arrange one-third of the slices to cover the bottom of a 13-by-9-inch baking dish. Spread 2 cups sauce over the slices. Scatter one-third of each cheese over the sauce. Repeat using one-third of the squash slices, 2 cups sauce and one-third of each cheese. Make a final layer with the remaining ingredients, ending with the cheese.

Cover the baking dish with aluminum foil and bake for 1 hour. Uncover the dish and continue baking for 20 to 30 minutes more, or until the casserole is browned and bubbly and the squash is tender when pierced with the tip of a knife. Remove from the oven and let sit for 10 to 15 minutes before cutting into squares and serving.

Braised Garlic *and* Buttercup Squash

Serves 4 to 6

SAVORY AND COMFORTING: These are the words that come to mind to describe this dish of cubed winter squash, whole garlic cloves, chicken stock and herbs. Don't worry about cutting the squash into uniform chunks; the thinner pieces cook down into a sort of puree, while the larger chunks stay whole. Try serving this as an alternative squash dish at your Thanksgiving table or with roast meat.

1 cup chicken stock

2 tablespoon unsalted butter

30 whole garlic cloves (approximately 2 heads), peeled

Freshly ground black pepper

Pinch of freshly ground nutmeg

2½-3 pounds buttercup, butternut or other orange winter squash, quartered, peeled, seeded and cut into 1-inch cubes

2-4 tablespoons mixed, chopped fresh herbs of choice, such as parsley, basil, thyme or sage, or 1 tablespoon dried mixed

Salt

Preheat the oven to 300 degrees F.

Place the stock, butter, garlic, pepper and nutmeg in a large ovenproof saucepan or Dutch oven. Bring to a boil and simmer the garlic, uncovered, for 10 minutes, or until slightly softened. Add the squash and herbs and toss to coat with the liquid.

Cover the pan and braise in the oven for 20 minutes. Stir the mixture and braise for 25 minutes more, or until the vegetables are very tender when pierced with the tip of a knife. If the squash pieces are very thick, the cooking time may need to be increased by 5 to 10 minutes.

When the squash is tender, transfer it and the garlic to a serving bowl with a slotted spoon. Reduce the liquid in the pan quickly over high heat until it is somewhat thickened. Correct the seasonings, adding salt and more pepper if needed. Pour the sauce over the squash and garlic, gently mix, then serve.

Pumpkin Cakes

Serves 4 to 6; makes 12 to 15 cakes

THIS IS A TAKEOFF on the Jewish latke, a potato pancake traditionally served at Hanukkah. I've replaced the usual grated white potatoes with grated pumpkin and seasoned the mixture with sage and nutmeg. The finished cakes are dusted with Parmesan cheese.

The batter may not look as though it will hold together, but it will. The lacy cakes are a pleasant change from pureed squash. I like serving them with pan-fried boneless chicken breasts that have been marinated in honey and Dijon mustard or with pan-roasted pork tenderloin and applesauce.

Grate the pumpkin on a medium-size grater and place in a medium bowl. Add the eggs, sage, nutmeg, salt and some pepper. Mix well with a fork.

Heat 2 tablespoons oil in a large skillet over medium-high heat. Drop heaping tablespoons of the pumpkin mixture into the pan and flatten into cakes. Cook until browned on both sides, 3 to 5 minutes per side. Transfer the cakes to a serving plate, keep warm and continue making cakes with the rest of the batter, using more oil as needed.

Sprinkle the cakes with Parmesan and serve.

1   pound pumpkin or other orange winter
      squash, quartered, peeled and seeded
3   large eggs
2   teaspoons minced fresh sage or
      1 teaspoon dried, crumbled
¼   teaspoon freshly ground nutmeg
¼   teaspoon salt
    Freshly ground black pepper
    Oil of choice, such as safflower,
      corn or vegetable, for frying
    Freshly grated Parmesan cheese

Chapter Four

Pasta

THE CAPACITY OF PASTA to make friends with nearly any ingredient in the kitchen means it is a cook's best ally where side dishes are concerned. For stews and braised dishes with generous amounts of gravy, pasta gives the plate a sense of completion as no other side dish can. Small wonder that many people accompany their beef stews with a homey dish of plain egg noodles.

One day, however, I wanted something

different. I boiled the noodles as usual, but re-membering a dish that is a specialty of the Burgundy region of France, I creamed together Dijon mustard, minced fresh parsley and garlic and a little melted butter. I seasoned the mixture with vigorous grindings of black pepper and tossed it with the noodles, adding some home-made croutons for a surprise crunch.

Whether the seasonings are strong and sturdy, like mustard and cream, or carefree and light, like ginger and mint, pasta goes with just about anything. Softer noodles make graceful accompaniments to stews. The understated flavors of baked pastas are good companions to spicy meals. For rich meats like duck, a pasta like Tubetini Pilaf with Cucumbers provides a welcome counterpoint. Other pasta dishes can be paired with main courses or stand alone; Pizzoccheri—hearty buckwheat noodles and greens layered with potatoes and fontina cheese—is an example.

After a conversation with a friend about food in the Dominican Republic, where green tomatoes are often served in salad, I started to wonder how a green-tomato sauce with basil and garlic would taste over pasta. Suggestive of lemons and apples, my experiment proved to be just right for serving alongside fish or chicken. On another day, I had the urge to mix spiral pasta and grilled celery. Somewhat later, I hit upon the whimsical idea of pairing strands of spaghetti squash with the pasta it resembles and mixing in some pesto as well. For butterfly pasta, I concocted a luxurious coating of caramelized onions and Gorgonzola, seasoned with caraway seeds to undercut some of the richness.

WHILE THE BEST-KNOWN pasta side dishes are soft ones, the textures can be nearly as various as the seasonings that go into them. Pasta can be crisp, as are vermicelli cakes with green tapenade, in which the noodles are mounded and pan-fried to a nutty brown. A humble gratin of angel hair pasta and cabbage depends for its effect on the contrast between the crunchy baked topping and the yielding interior. Sautéed in butter and simmered in broth, small pasta takes on a pilaf-like fluffiness.

For many of the recipes in this chapter, you can put together the garnishes while the pasta boils, making these dishes ideal for weekday cooking. Others, such as Pizzoccheri, take more time but repay the effort with dividends of flavor.

PASTA

Penne *with* Asparagus *and* Lemon

Serves 6

THIS IS AN ELEGANT combination of pasta tubes and asparagus cut on an angle, flavored with cream and lemon. Do not be afraid of adding the lemon juice directly to the cream. Stir the sauce continuously as you slowly pour it in and it will not curdle. Try to find thin to medium-sized asparagus stalks for this recipe. Serve with veal, chicken, turkey scallopini or fish.

1 pound medium asparagus, trimmed
Salt
½ pound penne pasta
1 tablespoon unsalted butter
2 large garlic cloves, minced
1 cup heavy cream
¼ cup fresh lemon juice
2 tablespoons chopped fresh parsley
2 teaspoons grated lemon zest
Freshly ground black pepper

Cut the asparagus into thirds on an angle; there should be about 4 cups. Set aside.

Bring a large pot of water to a boil. Add ½ tablespoon salt to the water and add the penne, stirring. Cook, stirring often, until it is tender yet firm and offers some resistance, 8 to 12 minutes.

While the pasta cooks, make the sauce. Melt the butter over low heat in a large nonreactive skillet. Add the garlic and stir to coat with the butter. Immediately add the asparagus and toss for 1 minute. Add the cream, raise the heat to high and bring to a boil. Boil for 3 minutes, or until the asparagus is crisp-tender and the cream has reduced. Remove from the heat. Slowly pour in the lemon juice, stirring constantly. Add the parsley, lemon zest, ¼ teaspoon salt and some pepper to taste; stir. When the pasta is done, drain well and add to the asparagus mixture. Stir well to mix the asparagus with the pasta. Taste for seasonings, adding more salt and pepper as needed. Serve immediately.

Variation

* Substitute an equal portion of thin green beans for the asparagus. You can also substitute zucchini, cut into half-moon slices. Sauté the slices in melted, unsalted butter over medium-high heat for 3 minutes to lightly brown them before adding the cream. Continue as directed.

Fusilli *with* Grilled Celery

Serves 4

I LOVE GRILLED CELERY, and it is a natural with pasta. Make this when you are planning to grill the main course or other foods. Alternatively, you can roast the celery during the winter.

6   celery stalks, rinsed, trimmed and dried
2-4 tablespoons olive oil
    Salt
    Freshly ground black pepper
½   pound fusilli, gemelli, rotini or
       any pasta twists
1   garlic clove, minced
¼   cup freshly grated Parmesan cheese

Prepare the grill by lighting the coals.

When the coals are ready (there should be no flames, just glowing red coals with a layer of gray ash around them), brush the celery with oil on both sides and grill for 2 to 3 minutes per side, 6 to 8 inches from the coals, until browned and softened with a bit of crunch. Transfer to a cutting board and cut the celery on an angle into pieces about the same size as the pasta. Transfer to a large serving bowl and season with a pinch of salt and some pepper; set aside.

Bring a large pot of water to a boil. Add ½ tablespoon salt to the water, add the pasta and stir. Cook, stirring often, until it is tender yet firm and offers some resistance, 8 to 10 minutes; drain. Transfer to the bowl with the celery and add the garlic. Toss everything together and taste for seasonings. Season with more salt and pepper if needed, sprinkle the cheese over the top of the dish and serve.

Variations

* You can roast the celery at 400 degrees F instead of grilling. Turn the celery after 20 minutes, cooking for a total of about 45 minutes.

* Grill trimmed, cleaned leeks along with the celery and add to the dish.

* Top the pasta with feta cheese in place of the Parmesan cheese.

* Add basil and chopped green olives at the end and perhaps some capers.

Tubetini Pilaf *with* Cucumbers

Serves 4

THE PASTA IN THIS DISH is prepared in the manner of rice pilaf. Tubetini—small tubular noodles—are sautéed in butter while still raw, then simmered in stock so that they become fluffy. They are then combined with lightly sautéed cucumbers. The process takes only about 15 minutes. This method allows you to experiment with many different garnishes, so change the cucumber to another ingredient, depending on the season. If tubetini is unavailable, use any small pasta, such as orzo or baby shells.

> 2 tablespoons unsalted butter
> 1 medium red onion (about 6 ounces), chopped
> Salt
> Freshly ground black pepper
> 1½ cups tubetini pasta
> 2 tablespoons chopped fresh tarragon or 2 teaspoons dried
> 1½ cups chicken or vegetable stock
> 1 large cucumber, peeled

Melt 1 tablespoon butter in a heavy pan over medium heat. Add the onion, ¼ teaspoon salt and some pepper, and sauté the onion, stirring, for about 3 minutes, or until it begins to lose its moisture and softens. Add the uncooked tubetini, stir and cook to heat the pasta. If using dried tarragon, add it now.

Pour in the stock, bring to a boil, reduce the heat to low, cover the pan and simmer for 10 to 15 minutes, or until all the stock is absorbed. Turn off the heat and leave covered for about 5 minutes until the pasta becomes tender.

Meanwhile, cut the cucumber lengthwise into quarters. Remove the seeds and cut lengthwise into ¼-inch-thick sticks. Cut the cucumber crosswise into ¼-inch dice. Melt the remaining 1 tablespoon of butter in a medium skillet over high heat. Add the cucumbers, a pinch of salt and some pepper, and cook about 3 minutes, tossing frequently, or until hot and beginning to soften but still crisp.

Mix the pasta and cucumbers in a medium serving bowl, and, if using fresh tarragon, add it now. Correct the seasonings, adding more salt and pepper if needed, and serve.

Variations

* Substitute 2 medium trimmed, cleaned leeks and thyme for red onion and tarragon. Use 4 ounces soft, mild goat cheese instead of the cucumbers, adding it after the pasta is cooked.

* Use other herbs, such as marjoram, chives, chervil, parsley, savory or thyme.

* Add roasted red pepper or diced tomato at the end of cooking.

* Minced garlic is a nice addition. Add with the onion.

* Finish the dish with boiled or steamed chopped artichoke hearts.

Two Spaghetti *with* Pesto

Serves 6 to 8

THIS DISH combines spaghetti and spaghetti squash in a cheesy, garlicky pesto sauce. I like the contrasting textures of the slightly crunchy spaghetti squash and the pasta. My son, Max, who is not a squash fan, consistently eats two or three servings of this uncomplicated dish.

If only large squash are available, buy one weighing about 3½ pounds, cook and use half in this recipe, reserving the other half for another use.

1   small spaghetti squash (about 2 pounds)

For the pesto

3   cups torn basil leaves

2   garlic cloves

¼   cup pine nuts, toasted (see page 22)

½   cup extra-virgin olive oil

¼   cup freshly grated Parmesan cheese

¼   cup freshly grated Romano cheese
    Freshly ground black pepper
    Salt

½   pound spaghetti

Preheat the oven to 375 degrees F.

Prick the spaghetti squash in a few spots and bake on the oven rack for about 1 hour, or until tender when pierced with the tip of a knife. Remove from the oven and cool a few minutes.

Meanwhile, make the pesto: Place the basil, garlic and nuts in a blender or food processor and puree. Add the oil and blend just to mix. Transfer the mixture to a bowl and stir in the cheeses and pepper, and salt if needed (taste first: the cheeses are salty). Set aside.

Bring a large pot of water to a boil. Add ½ tablespoon salt to the water and add the spaghetti, stirring. Cook, stirring often, until it is tender yet firm and offers some resistance, 8 to 10 minutes. Cut the squash in half lengthwise. Scrape out the seeds and scoop the squash into a large serving bowl. Break up the squash with a fork. Add half the pesto and mix it into the squash evenly.

When the spaghetti has cooked, drain and transfer to the bowl with the spaghetti squash. Add the remaining pesto and toss. Taste for seasonings, adding more salt and pepper if needed, and serve.

Fettuccine *with* Green Tomato Sauce

Serves 4 to 6

GREEN TOMATOES have a bright lemony flavor that nicely balances the fettuccine. The tomatoes need to be slightly ripe, yellow or with a slight blush. Hard, solidly green tomatoes will not work as well, for they are too acidic. Serve with broiled scallops or other fish dishes or with chicken or pork tenderloin.

¼ cup olive oil

2 large garlic cloves, minced

⅓ cup chopped fresh parsley

2 pounds slightly ripe green tomatoes
     (yellow or with a slight blush
     on the shoulders), cored and
     cut into wedges

   Salt

   Freshly ground black pepper

2 tablespoons chopped fresh basil or
     2 teaspoons dried

1 pound dried fettuccine

Warm the oil over low heat in a large nonreactive skillet or Dutch oven. Add the garlic and sauté for 2 minutes, or until slightly softened, without allowing it to color. Add the parsley and sauté for 1 minute more. Add the tomato wedges, ½ teaspoon salt and some pepper, stir well and raise the heat to medium. Cook, covered, for 10 minutes to soften the tomatoes and release their moisture, stirring a few times.

Uncover and cook for 20 minutes more to reduce the sauce, stirring and breaking up the tomatoes as they cook. Reduce the heat to medium-low, then to low, so the sauce will not burn as it reduces and thickens. Add the basil and correct the seasonings, adding more salt and pepper if needed.

Meanwhile, bring a large pot of water to a boil. Add 1 tablespoon salt to the water and add the fettuccine, stirring. Cook, stirring often, until it is tender yet firm and offers some resistance, 6 to 8 minutes; drain. Place in a large bowl and top with the green tomato sauce. Mix gently and serve.

Variations

* Serve this sauce on spaghetti squash.
* Serve on spaghetti mixed with spaghetti squash.

Curried Orzo Risotto Style

Serves 6

PICTURE A SAVORY RICE PUDDING flavored with curry, cream, chicken broth and tiny peas. Substitute orzo pasta for the rice, and borrow the method for the Italian dish risotto, stirring the pasta continuously in an open pan, and you end up with this luscious dish. Although cooking risotto does require constant stirring, the orzo cooks quickly, so you will not be tied to the stove for long. Serve with chicken, fish or lamb, along with a salad of mixed greens and sweet cherry tomatoes.

1	cup tiny peas, fresh or frozen
	Salt
2	tablespoons unsalted butter
1	medium onion, chopped
½	pound orzo (rice-shaped pasta)
2	teaspoons curry powder
1½	cups chicken stock
1½	cups light or heavy cream
	Freshly ground black pepper

If using fresh peas, blanch in a small saucepan of boiling, salted water for 1 to 2 minutes, drain, rinse under cold water, drain again and set aside. If using frozen peas, thaw and set aside.

Melt the butter in a medium saucepan over medium-high heat. Add the onion and sauté for about 5 minutes, or until it begins to lose its moisture. Add the orzo and stir. Cook the orzo to color it lightly, about 2 minutes, tossing frequently. Add the curry powder and cook for 1 minute more, tossing.

Add ½ cup stock and stir until it is completely absorbed. Repeat with ½-cup additions, using all the stock first, then adding the cream in ½-cup additions, stirring the dish continuously during the cooking. Cook until the dish is very creamy and appears custardlike and the pasta is tender, with a slight resistance, 10 to 15 minutes.

Season well with salt and pepper, stir in the reserved peas and serve immediately.

Variations

* Add minced fresh ginger with the curry and grated lime zest at the end of cooking. Replace ¼ cup of the chicken stock with lime juice.

* Try using unsweetened coconut milk in place of the cream. Top the dish with sliced, toasted almonds (see page 22).

* Replace the peas with blanched green beans cut into ½-inch pieces, or with spinach, blanched fava beans, diced tomato or a mixture of blanched green beans and diced tomato.

Ginger Orzo Salad

Serves 6 to 8

COOKED ORZO is mixed with shredded radishes and carrots and tossed with a ginger-mint dressing. The salad is then left to chill and marinate.

This salad is terrific to carry along on a picnic. Make it early in the morning or the day before to give the pasta a chance to absorb all of the flavors.

1 bunch or 1 bag radishes
(8-10 ounces), trimmed

2 large carrots, peeled and trimmed

1 2-inch piece fresh ginger (about
1 ounce), peeled and sliced

¼ cup fresh lemon juice

¼ cup olive oil

¼ cup extra-virgin olive oil
Salt
Freshly ground black pepper

¼ cup chopped fresh mint or
1 tablespoon dried

2 cups orzo (rice-shaped pasta)

Bring a large pot of water to a boil.

Shred the radishes and carrots in a food processor or a mouli grater, using the medium julienne disk, or on a hand grater. Set aside.

Place the ginger, lemon juice, oils, ½ teaspoon salt and some pepper in a blender. Puree until smooth. Add the mint and puree until the dressing begins to turn pale green. Set aside.

Add 2 teaspoons salt to the boiling water, add the orzo and stir. Cook, stirring often, until it is tender yet firm and offers some resistance, 7 to 10 minutes. Drain and rinse under lukewarm water. Drain well and place in a large bowl.

Add the reserved radishes and carrots to the bowl with the orzo. Whisk and taste the dressing for seasonings, adding more salt and pepper if needed. Pour over the salad and toss well to coat. Marinate in the refrigerator until ready to serve. Serve chilled.

Egg Noodles *with* Mustard *and* Croutons

Serves 4

THE IDEA FOR THIS DISH comes from the city of Dijon in France, where mustard is honored and savored. In this area of France, known as Burgundy, noodles with butter and Dijon mustard accompany the classic stew, *boeuf bourguignon.* I have added garlic and delightfully crisp croutons to the soft dish. Serve with beef stew, roast chicken, baked ham, lamb chops or pan-fried steak.

¼ cup Dijon mustard

¼ cup chopped fresh parsley

2 garlic cloves, minced

2 tablespoons unsalted butter, softened
Freshly ground black pepper
Salt

½ pound wide egg noodles

1½ cups croutons, preferably homemade, lightly crushed

Place the mustard, parsley, garlic, butter and pepper in a small bowl. Cream together with a fork until all the ingredients are homogenous.

Bring a large pot of water to a boil. Add ½ tablespoon salt to the water, then add the egg noodles and stir. Cook, stirring often, until the noodles are tender yet firm and offer some resistance, 6 to 8 minutes; drain.

Place the noodles in a large bowl and add the butter-parsley mixture. Toss well to coat the pasta. Add the croutons and toss again to distribute them evenly. Correct the seasonings, adding more salt and pepper if needed, and serve.

Farfalle *with* Gorgonzola

Serves 4 to 6

THIS IS A RICH DISH with a wonderful melding of sweet, salty and savory flavors. The onions provide sweetness, and the blue cheese and caraway contribute salt and spice, respectively. The onions take 30 to 45 minutes to cook, so allow a little extra time. Serve with roast chicken.

1 tablespoon unsalted butter
1 tablespoon olive oil
1 pound onions, sliced
  Salt
  Freshly ground black pepper
1 teaspoon caraway seeds
½ pound farfalle pasta (butterflies)
¼ pound Gorgonzola cheese (if unavailable, use Blue Castello or Saga blue cheese)
1 tablespoon chopped fresh parsley
1 tablespoon snipped fresh chives

Heat the butter and oil in a large skillet over medium heat. Add the onions, ¼ teaspoon salt and some pepper and toss to coat the onions. Cook the onions for 30 to 45 minutes, or until they are soft and brown, adding the caraway seeds after 30 minutes.

After the onions have cooked for 15 to 20 minutes, bring a large pot of water to a boil. Add ½ tablespoon salt to the water in the pot and add the pasta, stirring. Cook, stirring often, until it is tender yet firm and offers some resistance, 8 to 12 minutes.

Drain the pasta and place in a large serving bowl. Add the onions, cheese, parsley and chives; mix well until the cheese melts. Taste for seasonings, adding more salt and pepper if needed, and serve.

Pizzoccheri

Serves 6 to 8

THIS RUSTIC, FILLING DISH from the Italian-Swiss Alps incorporates buckwheat pasta with potatoes, greens and cheese. It is great after a hike on a cold day.

3   tablespoons unsalted butter
1   Spanish onion (about 1 pound),
        sliced ⅓ inch thick
    Salt
    Freshly ground black pepper
2   tablespoons chopped fresh parsley
2   tablespoons snipped fresh chives
½   pound buckwheat noodles,
        fettuccine-style
1   bunch Swiss chard, washed,
        dried and torn into pieces
½   pound all-purpose potatoes,
        peeled and thinly sliced
3   cups grated Italian fontina cheese

Melt 2 tablespoons of the butter in a large skillet over medium heat. Add the onion and season with ¼ teaspoon salt and some pepper. Cook, stirring often, until the onion is browning well, 20 to 30 minutes. Add the herbs, mix well and set aside.

Meanwhile, bring a large pot of water to a boil. Add ½ tablespoon salt to the water, add the pasta and stir. Cook, stirring often, until the pasta is softened but not cooked through, 5 to 8 minutes. (The pasta will finish cooking in the oven.) Drain and add to the onion mixture. Toss well and set aside.

Preheat the oven to 350 degrees F.

Melt the remaining 1 tablespoon butter in a large skillet over high heat. Add the chard, cover and cook, uncovering and stirring, until just barely wilted, 2 to 5 minutes. Transfer the cooked chard to a 13-by-9-inch baking dish. Spread to form an even layer. Set aside.

Place the potatoes in a medium saucepan and cover with cold water. Bring to a boil and cook for 5 minutes, or until slightly softened. Drain, season with ¼ teaspoon salt and some pepper and stir into the pasta mixture, breaking up the slices.

Scatter half the cheese over the chard, then spread the pasta mixture over the cheese. Top with the remaining cheese. Bake until bubbly and golden on top, 20 to 30 minutes. Let stand for about 10 minutes before serving.

Fried Vermicelli Cakes *with* Green Tapenade

Serves 4; makes 8 cakes

MY FRIEND AND COLLEAGUE Linda Marino introduced me to these delightful cakes, which are made with cooked pasta browned in oil, similar to rice or potato pancakes. I love their crisp nutty exterior and soft interior. Linda often makes them for her family when she is serving seafood, spreading them with anchovy butter. I top them with a dollop of homemade tapenade, a Provençal spread made with green olives instead of the usual black. Mixed with butter, the topping melts and forms a sauce. Serve with tuna, swordfish or whitefish.

The tapenade recipe makes about 1½ cups—more than you will need for this dish. But it keeps for several months stored in the refrigerator, and it's wonderful on toast, croutons or bruschetta. If you are in a hurry, use minced green olives by themselves in place of the tapenade.

For the tapenade

1 cup pitted green olives
8 anchovy fillets
2 garlic cloves, coarsely chopped
1 tablespoon drained capers, rinsed and drained again
½ cup extra-virgin olive oil
1½ tablespoons unsalted butter, softened
Freshly ground black pepper

For the vermicelli cakes
Salt
½ pound vermicelli
Olive oil

To make the tapenade: Combine the olives, anchovies, garlic and capers in a food processor or blender and puree. You can also chop them finely with a knife or crush them together using a mortar and pestle. Add the oil in a steady stream, whisking until smooth.

Place the butter and 1½ tablespoons tapenade in a small bowl. (Store the remaining tapenade in the refrigerator.) Grind in some pepper and mix with a fork or rubber spatula until homogenous. Taste and add more pepper, if desired. Set aside.

To make the cakes: Bring a large pot of water to a boil. Add ½ tablespoon salt to the water, add the vermicelli and stir. Cook, stirring often, until it is tender yet firm and offers some resistance, about 6 minutes.

When the pasta is done, drain it and either return it to the pot or transfer it to a large bowl. Add 1 tablespoon oil and toss to coat the pasta so that it does not stick together.

Heat another 1 tablespoon oil in a large skillet over medium heat. Divide the pasta into 8 roughly equal portions; it does not matter if some cakes are larger than others. Using a fork, twirl a serving of pasta and place in the skillet. Repeat, making 3 more cakes. Brown the cakes for about 3 minutes per side.

Transfer the cakes to a platter and keep warm while you brown the remaining cakes. Season the cakes with salt and pepper, and spoon a dollop of tapenade butter on each cake. The heat of the cake will melt the butter to create a sauce. Serve warm, allotting 2 cakes per person.

Variation

* Top the cakes with some minced celery.

Baked Angel Hair *and* Cabbage

Serves 6 to 8

THIS HEARTY DISH of sautéed cabbage, rosemary and cooked angel hair pasta is best when prepared with savoy cabbage, but can be made with the ordinary green kind. Serve with salad and fruit for a meal in itself or with chicken, lamb or fish.

1 savoy cabbage (about 2 pounds)
4 tablespoons olive oil
  Salt
  Freshly ground black pepper
4 large garlic cloves, minced
2 tablespoons chopped fresh rosemary
    or 2 teaspoons dried, crumbled
½ pound angel hair pasta
1 cup chicken or vegetable stock
1 cup fresh bread crumbs

Quarter and core the cabbage. Slice crosswise into thin slices. Heat 2 tablespoons of the oil in a large Dutch oven over medium heat. Add the cabbage, ¼ teaspoon salt and some pepper, and toss. Cover and cook for 10 minutes. Uncover, add garlic and rosemary, toss, cover again and continue cooking 10 to 15 minutes more, until the cabbage is soft and wilted.

Meanwhile, preheat the oven to 350 degrees F.

Bring a large pot of water to a boil. Add ½ tablespoon salt, then add the pasta, stirring, and cook, stirring, for 2 minutes, until it is softened. Drain and toss with the remaining 2 tablespoons oil and salt and pepper to taste.

Mix the pasta with the cabbage, using 2 forks, and transfer to a 14-by-10-by-3-inch baking dish or a lasagna pan. Pour in the stock. Sprinkle with the bread crumbs and bake for 45 minutes, or until golden. Let sit for 10 minutes to set up, and serve.

Variations

* For a main dish, split a 3-to-4-pound chicken through the backbone and flatten, then place on top of the pasta. Bake for 45 minutes to 1 hour. Or place a salmon fillet on the pasta during the last 15 to 20 minutes of baking. Or top with a small lamb shoulder or half a leg and cook for 45 minutes to 1 hour.

* Substitute savory, thyme or Provençal herbs for rosemary.

Chapter Five

Potatoes

M Y FAMILY is from New England—New Hampshire millers, with strong roots in the country. When it came to choosing a starch for dinner, it was potatoes, plain and simple. We ate them in all sorts of ways: baked, mashed, scattered around the Sunday roast or French-fried. More often than not, though, we ate them boiled. Best of all were the mashed potatoes, with plenty of salt and butter, served with an extra square of butter in a little well made with the back of the spoon. Gravy was for special occasions, holidays or Sundays.

My master recipe for mashed potatoes is still the one I loved as a child. But my variations travel far from the butter and gravy that were once the sole embellishments of my favorite side dish. Sometimes, I mash potatoes with sweetly caramelized roast garlic—either whole cloves or puree. On another day, I scatter crumbled bacon on the soft peaks. Or I toss in some sautéed leeks or a pungent burst of garlic that I've chopped together with fresh parsley. With pesto, sautéed mushrooms, greens, all manner of fresh herbs, cheeses (from Gorgonzola to ricotta), sun-dried tomatoes and black olives or other cooked vegetables like turnips, it's no wonder that my mashed potatoes fit in with any meal. For baked potatoes, too, the toppings are nearly as wide-ranging: lean and feisty (salsa), pungent and exploding with flavor (olives and capers) or hearty and filling (cooked pinto beans and sour cream).

The potato encourages freewheeling behavior in the kitchen, for although its earthy and relatively neutral character shines with butter, it also invites sweet, spicy, aromatic and even tart flavors. A completely classic gratin of potatoes, the French version of scalloped potatoes, with its rich dose of heavy cream, is an indulgence. Kevin's Barbecued Potato Salad marries sweet,

vinegary and spicy barbecue sauce to smooth red potatoes. From there, it's a short skip to Potato and Cranberry Pie, another gratin, this one delightfully unconventional: The potatoes cozy up to curry powder and cranberries with surprising naturalness.

WHILE POTATOES have an easygoing nature that makes them almost infinitely versatile, they are not all built alike. Varieties range from smooth and waxy to mealy and starchy. Waxy potatoes, such as reds and California new potatoes, are low in starch. Drier potatoes, such as russets or Idahos, are high in starch, and their texture is mealy. All-purpose potatoes, Yellow Finns and Yukon Golds fall somewhere in between.

New, waxy potatoes are best for grilling, steaming or boiling because they hold their shape better. If you try to boil a starchy potato for a salad, it will fall apart. I also prefer preparing mashed potatoes with waxy varieties, since they do not need as much liquid enrichment, and their finished consistency is less thick and pasty. Some other cooks, however, like to use all-purpose or starchy types.

The starchier potatoes, such as russets, are

best for baking, oven-roasting or frying. This is because their starches swell and absorb the steam created from the moisture sealed inside the skin or the browned outer layer, producing a dry and fluffy texture.

All-purpose potatoes, as their name implies, lend themselves well to baking, frying, boiling, grilling, oven-roasting, steaming and even mashing. I don't recommend them for salads, since they do not hold their shape and are grainy.

This chapter also contains recipes for the kissing cousin to the potato, the sweet potato. The preparation techniques are similar to those for ordinary spuds. Recipes include mashed sweets with onions, home-fries with cayenne and a sweet-potato casserole that gives the sugary orange flesh a jab of lime. All of these imaginative renditions make potatoes anything but routine.

POTATOES

Grilled Summer Home Fries

Serves 6

THIS ALTERNATIVE TO HOME FRIES combines grilled red potatoes, red onions and corn. The smoky vegetables are cut into large pieces when done and seasoned with garlic and herbs. These potatoes are particularly delicious with steak, sausages or egg dishes. Try them also with grilled meats, poultry or fish.

1 pound medium-size red potatoes
   of uniform size, unpeeled
   Olive oil
2 medium-size red onions,
   cut into ⅓-inch-thick slices
4 ears sweet corn, husks and silks
   removed
2 large garlic cloves, minced
2 tablespoons chopped fresh mint
   or thyme or 2 teaspoons dried
   Salt
   Freshly ground black pepper

Prepare the grill by lighting the coals.

Bring the potatoes to a boil in a medium or large pot of water and cook 5 to 7 minutes, or until barely tender. Drain. When the potatoes are cool enough to handle, cut into ⅓-inch-thick slices and brush with oil to coat. Set aside on a large plate.

When the coals are ready (there should be no flames, just glowing red coals with a layer of gray ash around them), brush all the onion slices and the ears of corn with the oil. Grill the potatoes, onions and corn, 6 to 8 inches from the coals, until browned, starting with the onion slices, since they take the longest to cook. Grill the onions for 5 to 7 minutes per side, or until just slightly resistant when pierced with the tip of a knife. Grill the potatoes for 5 minutes per side, or until soft when pierced with the tip of a knife. Grill the corn for 3 to 5 minutes, turning often.

As the onions and potatoes finish cooking, transfer them to a cutting board and cut into large pieces. Place in a large bowl. Cut the corn from the cob and add to the bowl. Add the garlic and herb of choice and a few tablespoons oil to coat the vegetables. Sprinkle with salt and pepper to taste and toss everything together. Serve immediately.

Kevin's Barbecued Potato Salad

Serves 6 to 8

AFTER YEARS OF EATING what is perhaps his favorite meal—barbecued spare ribs and potato salad—my friend Kevin suggested making the salad with the barbecue sauce left in the dish, since he had been mixing the two on his plate forever. The resulting salad was smoky, sweet-spicy and creamy. The potatoes can be steamed or wrapped in foil and cooked on the grill for a smokier taste.

I bake my ribs in a pan in the oven and use the leftover sauce for the salad after the meat has cooked. This recipe makes 1 to 1¼ cups finished sauce; you will have extra to freeze.

Serve with barbecued pork ribs, chicken, turkey, ham, hamburgers, turkey burgers or fish.

For the barbecue sauce

- 1 tablespoon corn or safflower oil
- 1 small onion, minced
  Salt
  Freshly ground black pepper
- 1 tablespoon minced garlic
- 1 teaspoon chili powder
- 1 teaspoon paprika
- ¼ teaspoon cayenne pepper
- 1½ cups tomato sauce of choice
- ¼ cup molasses (any kind)
- 2 tablespoons cider vinegar
- 1 tablespoon Dijon-style mustard
- ½ teaspoon Tabasco sauce
- ½ teaspoon Worcestershire sauce

For the potatoes

- 2 pounds baby red or small California new potatoes, scrubbed
- 3 tablespoons corn or safflower oil
- 1 tablespoon cider vinegar
  Salt
  Freshly ground black pepper

- ½ cup mayonnaise

To make the sauce: Heat the oil in a small non-reactive saucepan over medium heat. Add the onion, season with ¼ teaspoon salt and some pepper and cook, stirring, 3 to 5 minutes, or until the onion begins to soften and lose its moisture. Add the garlic and cook 1 minute, stirring, to soften slightly. Add the chili powder, paprika and cayenne. Mix and cook 1 minute more to heat the spices. Add the tomato sauce, molasses, vinegar, mustard, Tabasco and Worcestershire sauce. Bring to a boil, reduce the heat to medium-low and simmer for 45 minutes to 1 hour, or until the sauce has reduced to 1 to 1¼ cups. Set aside.

Meanwhile, cook the potatoes: Place them in a steamer basket over boiling water, cover and steam until tender, 10 to 15 minutes depending on their size. If you prefer, you can grill them: Light the coals. When they are ready (there should be no flames, just glowing red coals with a layer of gray ash around them), wrap the potatoes in 2 layers of foil and grill, 6 to 8 inches from the coals, until tender, 10 to 15 minutes.

When the potatoes are done, cut them in half and place in a large serving bowl. Add the oil, vinegar, ½ teaspoon salt and some pepper. Toss the potatoes well in the dressing to coat them, and set aside to cool while the sauce finishes cooking.

When the sauce is done, measure ¾ cup and place in a small bowl. Add the mayonnaise and whisk together. Pour the sauce over the reserved potatoes and mix well to coat. Correct the seasonings with salt and more cayenne or Tabasco as needed. Serve at room temperature or chilled.

Variation

*Try this dish with steamed or grilled sweet potatoes. Make the sauce with lemon juice in place of the vinegar and add minced candied ginger, and substitute lemon juice for the vinegar in the potatoes.

Mashed Potatoes *and* Variations

Serves 2 to 4

I HEAD FOR THIS DISH when I'm having a low day or if stress settles in. Mashed potatoes become gummy when made in the mixer or food processor. Mash only with a fork, food mill, ricer or masher. If you like lumps, the best equipment is a fork or a masher. Warming the liquid is essential as well. Cold liquid will gel the starches and the potatoes will be heavier. When mixing in the warmed liquid, do so gently, just to combine. I've given a basic recipe here; the rest is up to you.

1 pound red potatoes or California new
   potatoes (or substitute Yukon Gold
   or Yellow Finns)
½ cup milk, half-and-half, cream or
   buttermilk (buttermilk is lower in fat
   and has a pleasant lemony-tart taste)
1-4 tablespoons unsalted butter
   Salt
   Lots of freshly ground black pepper
   Freshly ground nutmeg to taste (optional)

Peel and rinse the potatoes and cut into 1½-to-2-inch chunks. Place them in a medium pot and cover with lots of cold water. Bring to a boil and cook until tender, 10 to 15 minutes depending on the size of the chunks; larger pieces may take up to 18 minutes.

While the potatoes cook, warm the liquid with as much butter as you like. Mash or rice the potatoes and pour in the warmed liquid. Add salt, pepper and nutmeg as needed, and mix everything just to combine. Serve as is or with other additions (see below).

Variations

* With leeks: Trim 1 bunch leeks (3 to 4) down to the white and light green parts. Cut each leek in half lengthwise and clean well under cold running water. Slice and sauté the slices in some butter with salt and pepper, adding thyme if you like, over medium heat for about 10 minutes, or until soft and browned. Mix into the mashed potatoes.

* With garlic, four ways: 1. Throw a bunch of peeled garlic cloves into the pot with the potatoes while they cook; mash together with the potatoes.

98

2. Roast the garlic until it is soft and tender, and mix the whole cloves into the finished mashed potatoes. You can roast the whole peeled cloves first, tossing them with olive oil. Or roast the whole head, first slicing off the tips of the cloves and rubbing them with olive oil, then pop out the roasted cloves and mix them into the finished potatoes. You can leave the cloves whole or mash them with the potatoes.

3. Make a big pile of persillade—chopped garlic and parsley—and mix into the finished potatoes. The flavor will be strong, since the garlic is raw.

4. Slice raw garlic thinly, sauté gently in a mixture of unsalted butter and olive oil until golden but not brown and scatter the chips over the top of each portion of potatoes.

* Mix mashed potatoes with pesto (page 80) and heavy cream.

* Mix with roasted garlic and crisp crumbled bacon.

* Mix with roasted garlic, crisp crumbled bacon and sautéed greens, such as Swiss chard, kale, mustard greens, escarole or broccoli rabe.

* Brown some mushrooms in unsalted butter and flavor with thyme and lemon juice. Serve on top of or mixed into the mashed potatoes.

* Herbs: Mix and match or use one alone. Some favorites are fresh basil, parsley, dill, marjoram, thyme, sage, rosemary, chives or chervil.

* Use extra-virgin olive oil instead of the butter. Try olive oil and lemon juice. Add herbs as well, if you like.

* Cheeses: Just about any cheese is great with potatoes. Try Gorgonzola, feta, goat, farmer, Cheddar, Parmesan, smoked cheeses, Gruyère, Monterey Jack or dry ricotta.

* Mix in sour cream or mascarpone.

* Top potatoes with crisply fried onion slices.

* Soften sun-dried tomatoes in hot water, drain and mix in, along with pitted black olives.

* Add a few tablespoons of mustard to the liquid and mix with the potatoes.

* Mix with hot chilies, either roasted or not.

* Cook the potatoes with some celery root, rutabaga, turnip, parsnip or carrot for a two-vegetable puree.

* Don't forget delicious old-fashioned gravy.

Baked Potatoes *with* Many Toppings

Serves 4

THIS IS A MASTER RECIPE with lots of variations. While you bake the potatoes, mix the topping—either the black olives and capers below—or any of the suggested variations.

4 russet (Idaho) potatoes, 6 ounces each (or 8-16 ounces for hearty appetites; double the topping amounts)

½ cup olives, mixed or all black, pitted and cut into quarters

2 tablespoons drained capers, rinsed and drained again

2 tablespoons extra-virgin olive oil

2 garlic cloves, minced

1-2 tablespoons chopped fresh thyme or savory or 1-2 teaspoons dried

1 tablespoon fresh lemon juice
   Freshly ground black pepper
   Salt

Preheat the oven to 400 degrees F.

Scrub and prick the potatoes and bake about 45 minutes (longer for larger potatoes), or until tender when pierced with the tip of a sharp knife.

While the potatoes cook, mix all the remaining ingredients except the salt in a small bowl and set aside.

When the potatoes are done, split open, season with salt and pepper to taste, top with the olive mixture and serve.

Variations

* Change the herb to any that you like. Basil, chives and parsley are good choices.

* Sauté mushrooms, garlic and parsley in butter. You can also mix in some diced baked ham. Top the split potatoes with the mixture and add a dollop of sour cream, if desired.

* Mix cooked red or pinto beans with cumin and sour cream and serve over the potatoes.

* Top with salsa and sour cream or cottage cheese.

* Top with sun-dried tomato pesto (see page 116).

* Sauté some onions in butter. Add chopped hard-cooked egg, drained and rinsed capers and chopped parsley. Serve over the potatoes.

Roast Potatoes *with* Smoked Gouda

Serves 4 to 6

THESE POTATOES are baked with smoked Gouda cheese. The idea was inspired by the Swiss dish raclette, cheese melted by the fire and served with boiled potatoes. If you are fortunate enough to have a fireplace, cook the potatoes in a pan over the coals and scatter the cheese over the potatoes to melt in the heat of the fire. In the summer, cook the potatoes on the grill. Serve with roast chicken or grilled steak.

2   pounds California new potatoes, large reds, Yukon Golds or Yellow Finns, peeled and cut into quarters (1-to-2-inch chunks)

2   tablespoons olive oil
    Salt
    Freshly ground black pepper

¼   pound smoked Gouda or other smoked cheese, grated
    Chopped fresh herbs of choice, such as parsley, chives or thyme (optional)

Preheat the oven to 400 degrees F.

Toss the potatoes in a medium bowl with the oil, ¼ teaspoon salt and some pepper. Transfer to an 11-by-7-inch baking dish and roast, tossing every 20 minutes with a spatula to scrape up all the crust, until tender, about 1 hour.

Scatter the grated cheese over the roasted potatoes and cook for about 5 minutes more to melt the cheese. Sprinkle with some fresh herbs, if using, and serve.

Variations

* Sprinkle the finished dish with crumbled cooked bacon and snipped chives.

* Add peeled whole shallots to the potatoes and roast together. Add some stock at the end of roasting and reduce the stock over high heat to glaze the mixture. Omit the cheese.

* Add peeled whole garlic cloves to the potatoes and roast together. Or roast all three: potatoes, shallots and garlic. Glaze with the stock. Omit the cheese.

* Add lemon juice, minced garlic and oregano to the potatoes with the olive oil before cooking. Roast the potatoes and omit the cheese.

Potato and Cranberry Pie

Serves 6

THIS CASSEROLE IS FILLING and satisfying. Thin slices of potato are arranged in two layers. Sandwiched in between are onions and cranberries that have been sautéed in curry powder. The cranberries add a tartness that contrasts nicely with the heat of the curry. Like a pie crust, the neutral potato balances the intense filling. This pie is delicious warm, at room temperature or even cold the next day; it improves as it sits. Serve with poultry and pork or as a main course in a vegetarian meal. I particularly love this dish with fish, such as a simply poached fillet of white fish or salmon.

Buy cranberries when in season and freeze for use throughout the winter; they keep well.

4 tablespoons olive oil
1½ pounds all-purpose potatoes, peeled and thinly sliced
Salt
Freshly ground black pepper
2 medium onions, red or yellow, thinly sliced
2 tablespoons curry powder
1½ cups fresh cranberries
½ cup fresh bread crumbs

Preheat the oven to 400 degrees F.

Spread 1 tablespoon of the oil in an 8-inch pie pan. Arrange some of the potato slices in concentric circles over the bottom and around the sides of the pan, overlapping them; you will use slightly more than half of the potatoes. Sprinkle them well with salt and pepper.

Heat 2 tablespoons of the oil in a medium skillet over medium heat. Add the onions, ¼ teaspoon salt and some pepper. Cook, stirring often, for about 5 minutes, or until the onions lose their moisture and soften. Add the curry powder and stir well. Cook for 1 more minute to heat the curry, stirring. Add the cranberries and mix well. Spread the onion-cranberry mixture over the potatoes in the pie pan. Arrange the remaining potatoes over the top in concentric circles, covering the onion-cranberry layer completely. Season well with salt and pepper.

Place the bread crumbs in a small bowl and add the remaining 1 tablespoon oil. Mix well with a fork. Spread the crumbs over the potatoes.

Bake for 40 minutes, cover with foil and continue baking for 20 minutes more, or until the potatoes feel tender when pierced with the tip of a sharp knife. Uncover and cook for 5 to 10 minutes more if the potatoes are not yet tender. When they are done, remove from the oven and let stand for 15 minutes so the pie sets up. Cut into wedges and serve.

Variation

* You can add other vegetables to the onions, such as sliced fennel or celery, for a change of taste.

Gratin *of* Potatoes

Serves 6 to 8

THIS CLASSIC VERSION of a French potato gratin layers potatoes with cream and seasonings in a casserole. Nothing could be richer or simpler. Serve with roast tenderloin of beef or roast chicken, or enjoy the leftover gratin in the morning with fried or scrambled eggs.

 1 garlic clove, split

 ½ tablespoon unsalted butter

 3-4 large russet (Idaho) potatoes,
       peeled and sliced paper thin

   Salt

   Freshly ground black pepper

   Freshly ground nutmeg

 2-3 cups heavy cream

Preheat the oven to 300 degrees F. Rub a 13-by-9-inch baking dish with the cut side of the garlic halves and let dry; butter the baking dish.

Place 1 layer of potato slices in the dish, overlapping them. Season well with salt, pepper and nutmeg. Pour some cream over the surface of the potatoes to barely cover. Repeat with potatoes, seasonings and cream, making 2 more layers, for a total of 3 layers. The potatoes should be just covered with the cream, not completely submerged.

Bake for 1 to 1½ hours, or until the potatoes are golden brown on top, the cream is almost all absorbed and the potatoes are tender when pierced with the tip of a sharp knife. Remove from the oven and let stand so the gratin will be easier to cut, 10 to 15 minutes.

Variations

* Mix ¼ to ⅓ cup Dijon mustard into the cream and add to the gratin.

* Mix about 1 cup of sun-dried tomato pesto or regular pesto (see pages 116 and 80) into the cream.

* Replace half the cream with chicken stock and layer the potatoes with slices of Gruyère or Gouda cheese.

* Sauté some savoy cabbage in butter and season well with salt, pepper and nutmeg. Replace half the cream with chicken stock and layer the potatoes with the sautéed cabbage. Top with a mixture of fresh bread crumbs and cooked crumbled bacon.

Sweet Potato Fries

Serves 4

THESE ARE PLEASURABLY INSIDIOUS, and they won't last until mealtime unless you ban everyone from the kitchen while you are cooking. French fries are best when they are double-fried. The first frying cooks the potato until softened, and the second frying browns and crisps the outsides. You can keep the first batch warm in a low oven while you fry the rest, but do not salt the potatoes until they are all done because the salt will make them soggy. Serve with fried fish.

- 1 teaspoon salt
- ⅛ teaspoon ground coriander
- ⅛ teaspoon cayenne pepper or to taste
- 3 sweet potatoes (1¾-2 pounds total)
   Oil of choice for frying, such as safflower or vegetable

In a small bowl, mix the salt, coriander and ⅛ teaspoon cayenne, or more if desired. Set aside.

Peel the sweet potatoes and cut into ⅓-inch-thick sticks. Pour the oil into a large skillet to a depth of 1 to 1½ inches. Heat over medium-high heat until shimmering (350 degrees F, if you have a thermometer). Using a slotted spoon, skimmer or fryer basket, add half the potatoes to the oil and fry 3 minutes, until softened. Do not crowd the skillet or the potatoes will not sear well. Drain on towels and repeat with the remaining potatoes.

Reheat the oil to 375 degrees F.

Add half the potatoes and fry 4 to 5 minutes more, until brown and crisp. Drain on towels and repeat with the remaining potatoes. Drain, sprinkle all the potatoes with the spiced salt and serve.

Baked Sweet Potatoes *with* Maple *and* Lime

Serves 6 to 8

THIS CASSEROLE—sweet with a tart edge—is similar in construction to the potato gratin of France. Rounds of sweet potato and red onion are layered and baked with a piquant mixture of lime juice and grated lime zest. The casserole is served with a sauce of maple syrup, lime juice, cracked pepper and herbs. While wonderful as a side dish with chicken, pork, ham or duck, these sweet potatoes also make a great main course for a vegetarian meal. The casserole improves as it sits; do not hesitate to reheat in a low oven the next day.

½ cup fresh lime juice

½ cup water

1 cup plus 1 teaspoon pure maple syrup

½ tablespoon olive oil

3 medium-large sweet potatoes
(2½-3 pounds total), peeled
and cut into paper-thin slices
Salt

2 large red onions (about 2 pounds total),
cut into paper-thin slices

1 teaspoon (packed) grated lime zest

1 cup fresh bread crumbs

½ teaspoon coarsely ground black pepper

2 teaspoons chopped fresh marjoram
or sage or 1 teaspoon dried

Preheat the oven to 350 degrees F.

Place 2 tablespoons of the lime juice in a small nonreactive saucepan; set aside. Place the remaining 6 tablespoons lime juice in another small nonreactive saucepan, along with the water and 1 teaspoon of the maple syrup. Bring to a boil, lower the heat until the mixture gently boils and reduce the mixture to ½ cup, 10 to 15 minutes depending on the size of the pan.

While the lime mixture reduces, lightly coat a 13-by-9-inch baking dish with the oil. Arrange a layer of one-third of the sweet potatoes in the dish and sprinkle with salt. Arrange half the onion slices over the potatoes and season with salt. Make another layer of potatoes, a layer of the remaining onion and finally a layer of the remaining potatoes, seasoning each layer with salt.

Add the lime zest and a pinch of salt to the reduced lime-maple mixture. Whisk and pour over the potato-onion casserole. Scatter the bread crumbs evenly over the top. Cover and bake ½ hour. Uncover and continue baking 45 minutes to 1 hour more, or until the crumbs are golden and crusty and the tip of a sharp knife passes easily through the potatoes; they should be very tender. Let the dish stand for 10 minutes to set up before serving.

When ready to serve, add the remaining 1 cup maple syrup to the reserved lime juice along with the pepper and the herb of choice. Gently heat without boiling and remove from the stove. To serve, cut portions of the casserole and transfer to plates. Spoon the sauce over the dish and serve.

Mashed Sweet Potatoes
with Sweet Onions

Serves 4 to 6

THIS IS A NICE CHANGE from ordinary mashed potatoes and requires little more in the way of effort than sautéing onions. The potatoes are baked rather than boiled to concentrate their sweet flavor. Unlike white potatoes, sweet potatoes have enough moisture so they do not need milk when they are mashed. Serve with sausage, ham, crab cakes, pork, roast chicken or turkey.

4 sweet potatoes (2-2½ pounds total)
4 tablespoons unsalted butter
1 large sweet onion (1-1½ pounds),
   such as Vidalia, cut into
   ½-inch-thick slices
Salt
Freshly ground black pepper
Freshly ground nutmeg

Preheat the oven to 400 degrees F.

Wash and prick the potatoes in several places. Place directly on the oven rack and bake until tender when pierced with the tip of a knife, 45 minutes to 1 hour.

Meanwhile, melt 2 tablespoons of the butter in a large skillet over high heat. Add the onions and sprinkle with salt. Cook until the onion slices are brown and crisp, stirring often so as not to burn, and lower the heat to medium-high after they start to brown. This will take 10 to 15 minutes.

When the potatoes are cooked, remove and discard the skins and mash the potatoes in a medium saucepan with a fork, masher, ricer or food mill. Add the remaining 2 tablespoons of butter, and salt, pepper and nutmeg to taste. Add the onion slices and mix together. Correct the seasonings, adding more salt, pepper and nutmeg if needed, and serve.

Chapter Six

Grains

BEFORE I WENT TO PARIS, I harbored wildly romantic visions of passing the time in cozy bistros and swank three-star restaurants. But when I finally got there, it was a skinny little Moroccan restaurant with tightly packed tables and lots of noise that caught my heart. The scents in the restaurant were exotic and strange, yet welcoming. A strong aroma of cinnamon, pepper and countless other spices I couldn't identify enveloped and warmed me. The couscous I ordered came piled high in a pyramid surrounded by a moat of sauce, with glistening vegetables. On first bite, a thousand tiny, perfectly separate spheres burst in my mouth with sweet, spicy flavors. The grains were punctuated with well-cooked vegetables—exactly which ones I no longer remember—but the couscous was unforgettable.

By the time I left Paris, couscous had become a favorite of mine. Made from granular semolina, couscous comes from the starchiest section of the whole wheat berry—the endosperm. Like pasta, it has a neutral taste and gets along with many different ingredients. It shines in a spicy summertime yogurt-based salad, with spices that make a nod to the dish I first tasted in Paris: cinnamon, cayenne pepper, ginger and cardamom. Couscous is just as hospitable to other well-seasoned additions, like pesto made with sun-dried tomatoes.

Although grains like couscous, quinoa, bulgur, cornmeal and barley have nourished cultures all over the world for thousands of years, they have taken a back seat to pasta, potatoes and rice in our culture. Fortunately, that is changing as cooks realize that these grains are readily available, inexpensive and quick to prepare. Best of all, they offer something different to put at the side of the plate.

Quinoa's tiny beads are larger than those of couscous, yet when cooked, their texture is similarly dry and separate. Quinoa is a little more flavorful than couscous, with a delicate nutlike savor. While not a true grain (it is actually the fruit of a leafy plant), it is used as one and teams well with nuts, dried fruits and cooked vegetables. Ready in a flash—a mere 10 to 15 minutes—it is highly convenient. Quinoa with Roasted Vegetables, a caramelized mixture of chopped roasted carrots and shallots combined with a pilaf made from that grain, is a fine accompaniment to rich fish such as salmon, as well as roast meats, stews or braised dishes.

With its chewy consistency, bulgur is somewhat heartier than quinoa. It, too, has the advantages of cooking quickly and being versatile. Part of the whole wheat berry, bulgur is precooked, dried and cracked into a fine- medium- or coarse-grind. Bulgur is popular in Middle Eastern cooking, notably in the dish tabbouleh, and it goes well with tomato, lemon, mint and parsley. It also adapts easily to other Mediterranean ingredients such as garlic and olives and takes to nuts, sweet herbs, fresh and dried fruits, and vegetables such as celery, carrots, sweet and spicy peppers and onions. Bulgur can be subtle, as it is in a chilled version similar to Waldorf salad with apples, nuts and celery, or vigorous, as in a warm pilaf with black olives, prunes, sweet red peppers and scallions.

LIKE BULGUR AND THE OTHER GRAINS, cornmeal makes a satisfying, filling side dish. Corn Fritters with Maple Sauce dipped in a combination of cider and maple syrup are good for breakfast, but they are equally delicious with a traditional New England ham and bean supper, sausage or pan-fried chicken breasts. When I serve veal chops, scallopini or roasted quail, I accompany them with Baked Polenta, which takes longer to make than fritters and has a soft consistency. The recipe in this chapter layers the polenta with Italian cheeses. Try it, too, with your favorite tomato sauce, bitter greens softly cooked with garlic or well-sautéed artichoke hearts.

Barley, the heartiest of the grains, is a good partner for woodsy, dark ingredients such as browned mushrooms, as well as lighter flavors like sweet herbs and cream. It requires the longest cooking time—45 to 60 minutes—but is well worth the wait. Barley can be steamed, baked, prepared pilaf- or risotto-style or turned into stuffings, casseroles or salads. If you want to be an instant convert to this grain, try the sumptuous barley on page 124, which is cooked with cream, kale, leek and a pinch of nutmeg.

You should store grains in the refrigerator in either glass jars or airtight plastic bags. Grains are rich in oils and quickly turn rancid. And if your kitchen is as cramped as a Moroccan restaurant in Paris, buy smaller quantities whenever possible and continually replace them.

GRAINS

Steamed Couscous

Makes 2 to 2¼ cups

THIS METHOD PRODUCES couscous that is far superior in texture to the "instant" technique that calls for adding boiling water and letting the grain sit for 5 minutes. Make a double batch and keep in the refrigerator for a couple of meals; it is well worth the effort. The result is fluffy, not wet, and without lumps.

¾   **cup couscous**

    Water

1   **teaspoon oil**

Place the couscous in a medium bowl and pour about 2 cups water over it. Swirl to rinse, then drain the couscous in a mesh strainer. Return it to the bowl and let stand 15 minutes so it swells and absorbs the moisture. Toss with a fork and place the couscous in the top of a couscousière or in a colander that fits into a larger pot.

Fill the pot or couscousière with 2 inches of water, making sure that the colander does not touch the water. Cover and steam 20 minutes over medium heat. Return the couscous to the bowl and add 2 tablespoons water. Toss well with a fork to mix. Cover with a towel and let stand 10 minutes.

Add the oil and mix thoroughly with the fork. Return the couscous to the colander or couscousière, cover and steam for 20 minutes more, or until tender. Transfer back to the bowl and serve or, if serving cold, cool to room temperature and chill in the refrigerator.

Chilled Couscous *with* North African Flavors

Serves 4

DRAINED YOGURT has a texture similar to sour cream, and in this salad, it becomes the base for a dressing to which sweet and hot spices are added, along with oil and lemon juice. The dressing is mixed with the couscous and with diced tomato for extra juiciness. Serve with chicken, fish, pork, beef and especially lamb.

1 cup plain whole-milk yogurt
½ teaspoon ground coriander
¼ teaspoon ground ginger
¼ teaspoon turmeric
⅛ teaspoon cayenne pepper
⅛ teaspoon ground cumin seed
⅛ teaspoon ground cinnamon
⅛ teaspoon freshly ground nutmeg
  Generous pinch of freshly ground
    black pepper
  Salt

2 tablespoons olive oil
1 tablespoon fresh lemon juice
¾ cup uncooked couscous
2 tablespoons chopped fresh parsley
    or mint or 2 teaspoons dried
1 large tomato (6-8 ounces), cored and diced
  Lettuce leaves (optional)
  Sliced cucumbers (optional)

To drain the yogurt: Place a strainer over a small bowl and line it with a paper towel. Place the yogurt in the strainer and set aside to drain for 30 minutes to 1 hour, or until you have ½ cup thick yogurt. Discard the liquid and transfer the yogurt to the small bowl by rolling it out of the towel and scraping any extra off the towel with a rubber spatula.

Add all the spices, pepper, ¼ teaspoon salt, oil and lemon juice. Mix well and set aside in the refrigerator until ready to use.

Meanwhile, steam the couscous as directed on page 113; when it is done, you should have about 2 cups. Transfer to a medium bowl, cool to room temperature and chill in the refrigerator.

When the couscous is cold, add the reserved yogurt sauce, parsley or mint, and diced tomato. Mix all of the ingredients well with a fork. Let the dish marinate 1 to 2 hours in the refrigerator, then serve on a bed of lettuce surrounded by sliced cucumbers, if desired.

Variations

* Add 1 to 2 minced garlic cloves to the yogurt sauce.

* Add 2 to 4 tablespoons chopped scallion or finely diced zucchini to the sauce.

Couscous *with* Sun-Dried Tomato Pesto

Serves 4

THIS DISH IS A COLORFUL BLEND of steamed couscous and sun-dried tomato puree mixed with fresh pesto. Blanch the dried tomatoes and puree in a food processor or blender, then add them to pesto. You will have more than you need for this dish. However, the pesto keeps well in the refrigerator for several weeks, or you can freeze the mixture. It is delicious on top of cracked wheat, rice or risotto, pasta, potatoes, chickpeas, white beans, pizza, crostini or bruschetta, or in stuffed eggs mixed with mayonnaise.

This dish is good hot or chilled.

For the pesto

3 cups basil leaves

2 garlic cloves, quartered

¼ cup pine nuts, preferably toasted (see page 22)

¾ cup extra-virgin olive oil

¼ cup grated Parmesan cheese

¼ cup grated Romano cheese

Salt

Freshly ground black pepper

2 cups sun-dried tomatoes

¾ cup uncooked couscous

To make the pesto: Place the basil, garlic and nuts in a blender or food processor and puree. Add ½ cup of the oil and blend just to mix. Transfer the mixture to a bowl and stir in the cheeses, a pinch of salt if needed, and some pepper. Set aside.

Bring a medium pot of water to a boil and add the sun-dried tomatoes. Return to the boil and blanch 3 minutes. Drain and place the tomatoes in the blender or food processor with the remaining ¼ cup oil and puree. Add the reserved pesto mixture and blend to distribute the tomatoes evenly. Transfer to a medium bowl and set aside.

Steam the couscous as directed on page 113 (you should have about 2 cups), and place in a medium bowl. Add ½ to ¾ cup of the pesto mixture and mix with a fork. (Store the remaining pesto in the refrigerator.) Correct the seasonings, adding more salt, pepper and pesto to taste, and serve.

Couscous with Buttermilk and Zucchini

Serves 4

BUTTERMILK ADDS TANG, while sautéed zucchini and dill bring savory notes to steamed couscous. In the winter months, serve this warm; in the summer months, the dish is good chilled. Serve with fish or shellfish, chicken breasts or roasted or grilled lamb.

¾ cup uncooked couscous

1 tablespoon unsalted butter

1 small zucchini (about ¼ pound),
     trimmed and diced

   Salt

   Freshly ground black pepper

1 garlic clove, minced

¼ cup buttermilk

2 tablespoons chopped fresh dill

Steam the couscous as directed on page 113 (you should have about 2 cups), and keep warm.

Melt the butter in a small skillet over medium heat. Add the zucchini, a pinch of salt and some pepper and cook, stirring, about 5 minutes to brown. Add the garlic and cook 1 minute more, or until slightly softened.

Place the couscous in a medium serving bowl and add the zucchini mixture, buttermilk and dill. Toss well with a fork to combine. Correct the seasonings, adding more salt and pepper if needed, and serve.

Variation

* Substitute diced steamed green beans for the zucchini.

117

Quinoa *with* Roasted Vegetables

Serves 4 to 6

QUINOA IS SIMPLE TO MAKE and extremely nutritious. In this pilaf, cooked quinoa is mixed with roasted carrots and shallots. Start roasting the vegetables before you begin the quinoa; they take longer to cook and can be held while the grain simmers.

Rinse the quinoa thoroughly with water to remove any residual saponins, the naturally occurring, sticky, soaplike substances that may be left after the seeds are prewashed, scrubbed and packaged.

- 2 medium carrots (about 6 ounces), peeled and diced
- 6 shallots (4-5 ounces), peeled and diced
- 1 tablespoon olive oil
  Salt
  Freshly ground black pepper
- 1 cup quinoa
- 1½ cups chicken stock
- ¼ cup dry white wine
- ¼ cup fresh lemon juice
- 2 tablespoons unsalted butter

Preheat the oven to 400 degrees F.

Toss the carrots and shallots with the oil, salt and pepper in a medium bowl. Transfer to an 8-inch cake pan and roast 25 to 30 minutes, tossing every 10 minutes or so, until caramelized and soft.

Meanwhile, place the quinoa in a strainer and rinse thoroughly with water. Transfer the quinoa to a medium nonreactive saucepan and add the stock, wine and lemon juice. Bring to a boil, reduce the heat to low, cover and simmer 10 to 15 minutes, or until all the liquid is absorbed and the grains are translucent. Add the butter and roasted vegetables and toss. Correct the seasonings, adding more salt and pepper if needed, and serve.

Bulgur Pilaf

Serves 4

THIS WINTRY PILAF of bulgur (precooked cracked wheat) is infused with the scents and flavors of cranberry, orange and sweet spices. Bulgur comes in three different grinds: fine, medium and coarse. For the best texture, use the coarse bulgur in this recipe. If it is not available, buy what you can get. Serve during the cooler months with broiled or roast chicken, lamb, pork or at the Thanksgiving table.

- 2 tablespoons olive oil
- 1 medium onion, finely chopped
- 1 cup finely chopped celery
- 2 garlic cloves, minced
- 1 cup coarse bulgur
- ¼ cup dried cranberries
- 1 teaspoon grated orange zest
- 1 teaspoon Chinese five-spice powder
- 1 cup chicken stock, warmed
  Salt
  Freshly ground black pepper

Heat the oil in a small, heavy saucepan over medium-high heat. Add the onion, celery and garlic. Toss and cook for 3 to 5 minutes, until the onion loses its moisture and becomes translucent.

Add the bulgur and toss well. Cook, tossing frequently, until the bulgur is hot to the touch, 1 to 2 minutes. Add the cranberries, orange zest and five-spice powder. Mix well to combine.

Add the stock and bring to a boil. Reduce the heat to low, cover and simmer until the liquid has been absorbed and the grains are tender, 15 to 20 minutes. Remove from the heat and let stand 10 minutes so the grains absorb the steam in the pan. Uncover, correct the seasonings, adding salt and pepper if needed, toss the bulgur with a fork and serve.

Bulgur *and* Pasta Pilaf

Serves 4

THIS DISH EXCITES ALL the senses with its combination of bulgur, baby pasta, sweet red peppers, salty black olives and prunes. The method is that of a classic pilaf: vegetables are sautéed, grain and pasta are added and briefly sautéed, and finally the stock is added and everything is simmered until done. Coarse bulgur is ideal if it is available; if not, medium or fine works as well. You can also substitute orzo (rice-shaped pasta) for the shell pasta. While this dish is a knockout served hot, it is equally delicious cold, making it great picnic food.

2 tablespoons olive oil

1 medium onion, chopped

1 medium-size sweet red pepper, cored, seeded and diced

Salt

Freshly ground black pepper

½ cup small (baby) shell pasta (about 2 ounces)

½ cup coarse bulgur

1 cup chicken stock, warmed

12 pitted prunes, halved

24 pitted Greek black olives, brine-cured (about ½ cup)

¼ cup sliced scallion greens

¼ cup chopped fresh parsley

Lemon wedges for serving (optional)

Heat the oil in a medium saucepan over medium heat. Add the onion, red pepper, ¼ teaspoon salt and some pepper and sauté 3 to 5 minutes, or until the onion begins to lose its moisture.

Add the pasta shells and cook 2 minutes, stirring. Add the bulgur and cook 1 minute more. Add the stock and prunes and bring to a boil. Reduce the heat to low, cover and simmer 15 to 20 minutes, or until all the liquid has been absorbed and the pasta and bulgur are tender.

Using a fork, fluff the pilaf and mix in the olives, scallions and parsley. Cover and let stand 10 minutes so the grains absorb the steam in the pan. Toss again, correct the seasonings, adding more salt and pepper as needed, and serve with lemon wedges, if desired.

Variations

* Top the dish with toasted pine nuts (see page 22).

* Add capers to the finished dish.

* Combine the above two variations.

* Omit the prunes, olives and scallions and add sugar snap peas (halved and sautéed briefly) at the end of cooking. Also add toasted, chopped walnuts (see page 22) and Parmesan cheese, if desired.

* Sauté some minced garlic with the onion.

* Omit the prunes, olives and scallions; add sautéed artichokes and trimmed, cleaned leeks along with toasted, chopped hazelnuts (see page 22).

Waldorf Bulgur Salad

Serves 6 to 8

THIS SALAD is a variation on the classic Waldorf combination of apples, celery and walnuts. I've replaced the walnuts with toasted chopped hazelnuts. The colors of the dish are subdued, adding lovely soft pale greens and beiges to a plate or buffet.

1 cup fine or medium bulgur

4 tablespoons hazelnut oil or
    extra-virgin olive oil

1 cup hot water

1 cup chopped celery (about 2 large stalks)

1 cup chopped green apple (about 1 large)

½ cup hazelnuts, toasted, skinned
    and chopped (see page 22)

   Salt

   Freshly ground black pepper

6 tablespoons fresh lemon juice,
    or more if desired

2 tablespoons snipped fresh chives

Place the bulgur in a medium serving bowl and toss with 1 tablespoon of the oil. Add the hot water. Cover and let sit 1 hour, or until the grains swell and soften.

Add the celery, apple, hazelnuts, ½ teaspoon salt and some pepper, 6 tablespoons lemon juice, chives and the remaining 3 tablespoons oil. Toss to mix thoroughly. Marinate at least 1 to 2 hours in the refrigerator so the flavors blend.

When ready to serve, toss and correct the seasonings, adding more salt, pepper and lemon juice if needed, then serve.

Variations

* Replace the apple with diced sweet red pepper.

* Replace the celery with diced fennel.

* Replace the apple with dried blueberries and add them with the hot water.

* Replace the celery, apple and hazelnuts with pitted fresh cherries and green olives. Use olive oil rather than hazelnut oil.

Barley *with* Mushrooms *and* Dill

Serves 4 to 6

BARLEY AND MUSHROOMS usually find themselves together in a soup. I've transferred them to a deep, woodsy pilaf. The rich browns of this dish are set off by a dusting of chopped dill.

2 tablespoons unsalted butter

1 medium onion, chopped, or 1 large leek, trimmed, well rinsed and cut crosswise into ¼-inch slices
   Salt
   Freshly ground black pepper

10 ounces cultivated mushrooms, rinsed, trimmed and chopped

6 ounces portobello mushrooms, rinsed, trimmed and chopped

½ cup pearl barley

1 teaspoon paprika

1½ cups chicken stock

3 tablespoons chopped fresh dill
   Sour cream or yogurt (undrained or drained, see page 114), for serving (optional)

Melt the butter in a medium saucepan over medium heat. Add the onion or leek, a pinch of salt and some pepper and cook, stirring, for 3 to 5 minutes, or until the onion or leek begins to lose its moisture and softens. Add the mushrooms and ¼ teaspoon salt, cover and cook to release their juices, about 2 minutes. Uncover, raise the heat to high and cook to evaporate the juices, 3 to 5 minutes.

Add the barley and brown lightly, stirring, 2 to 3 minutes. Add the paprika and cook 1 minute more. Add the stock and bring to a boil. Reduce the heat to low and simmer, covered, for 50 to 60 minutes, or until all the liquid is absorbed and the barley is tender. Remove from the heat and let stand, covered, for 10 minutes so the barley absorbs the steam in the pan.

Mix in 2 tablespoons of the dill. Correct the seasonings, adding more salt and pepper if needed, and sprinkle the remaining 1 tablespoon dill over the top of the dish. Serve with sour cream or yogurt on the side, if desired.

Variation

* Add 1 teaspoon caraway seeds with the paprika.

Barley *with* Creamy Kale

Serves 4 to 6

THE KALE ADDS an earthy dimension to this pilaf, while cream smoothes and refines it.

2 tablespoons unsalted butter

1 large leek, trimmed, well rinsed and
    cut crosswise into ¼-inch slices

4 ounces kale leaves, rinsed and coarsely
    chopped (about 4 cups packed)

¼ teaspoon freshly ground nutmeg
    Salt
    Freshly ground black pepper

½ cup pearl barley

1 cup chicken stock

½ cup heavy or light cream

2 tablespoons chopped fresh
    parsley (optional)

Melt the butter in a medium saucepan over medium heat. Add the leek, kale, nutmeg and some salt and pepper, and cook 3 to 5 minutes, covered, to wilt the kale and soften the leek.

Uncover, add the barley and brown lightly, 2 to 3 minutes. Add the stock and cream, and bring to a boil. Reduce the heat to low or medium-low, cover and simmer for 50 to 60 minutes, or until all the liquid is absorbed and the barley is tender. Remove from the heat and let stand, covered, for 10 minutes so the barley absorbs the steam in the pan.

After the barley has rested, add the parsley, if desired. Correct the seasonings, adding more salt, pepper and nutmeg if needed, and serve.

Sage Cakes

Serves 4; makes 16 cakes

A PLAIN PANCAKE with chopped sage embodies the Shaker ideal of simplicity. As with all Shaker food, simplicity is synonymous with perfection: These cakes are heavenly. Serve them with sausage, roast pork, veal or chicken, or with applesauce and bacon for an old-fashioned Sunday night supper.

1 cup sifted flour

1 teaspoon sugar

½ teaspoon salt

2 large eggs, separated

1 cup buttermilk

3 tablespoons chopped fresh sage leaves
    or 3 teaspoons dried and crumbled

About 1 tablespoon each vegetable oil
    and butter to fry the cakes

Extra butter for serving (optional)

Grated Parmesan or Romano cheese
    (optional)

In a medium bowl, mix the flour, sugar and salt. Add the egg yolks, buttermilk and sage and mix well. Let the batter stand for 30 minutes so the starches swell and absorb the liquid.

Beat the whites until firm but not dry and fold into the batter. Heat ½ tablespoon each oil and butter in a large skillet over medium-high heat. Drop spoonfuls of batter into the hot skillet and cook until golden brown on both sides, 1 to 2 minutes each side. Transfer the cakes as they are done to plates or a platter. Repeat with the remaining batter, using more oil and butter as needed.

Spread the cakes with more butter and sprinkle with cheese, if desired. Serve hot.

Baked Polenta *with* Italian Cheeses

Serves 6 to 8

Polenta is cornmeal and liquid (water, stock or milk) cooked together until the mixture becomes so thick that a spoon can stand straight up in it. It can be served as a porridge, or it can be baked or cut into shapes and fried. Here, it is layered with a blend of Italian cheeses and heavy cream and then baked. Serve with chicken, small birds such as quail or squab, rabbit, veal stew or scallopini, or pan-fried veal chops.

Corn flour—finely ground cornmeal—is available in Italian markets.

½ tablespoon olive oil

1 cup cornmeal or ½ cup cornmeal and
  ½ cup corn flour (not cornstarch)

3 cups chicken stock: 1 cup cold,
  2 cups boiling

  Salt

  Freshly ground black pepper

½ teaspoon freshly ground nutmeg

4 tablespoons unsalted butter

2 large eggs, beaten

½ pound Italian fontina cheese,
  cut into slices

½ cup grated Parmesan cheese

¼ cup heavy cream

Preheat the oven to 400 degrees F. Oil a baking dish that will hold between 4 and 6 cups.

Place the cornmeal in a medium bowl, add the cold stock and mix well. Pour the boiling stock over the mixture, whisking continuously until the mixture is smooth and without lumps. Transfer the mixture to a heavy medium saucepan. Add ½ teaspoon salt, some pepper and the nutmeg.

Over medium heat, slowly bring the polenta to a boil, whisking. When it is boiling, reduce the heat to low, switch to a wooden spoon and cook, stirring continuously, until the polenta is thick enough to support a spoon. (To test for this, tilt the saucepan and scrape all of the polenta into the corner. Then stand the spoon up in the middle of the mixture.)

Rinse out the bowl that you mixed the cornmeal in and transfer the polenta to it. Add the butter and stir it in as it melts. Set aside to cool slightly. Correct the seasonings, adding more salt, pepper and nutmeg if needed.

Add the beaten eggs to the polenta, mixing constantly until they are incorporated. Pour half the polenta into the baking dish. Arrange half of the fontina slices over the polenta and sprinkle with half the Parmesan cheese. Spread the remaining polenta in the dish and top with the remaining fontina slices and the Parmesan cheese. Pour the cream gently over the cheeses.

Bake the polenta until it is bubbly and the top is golden brown, 20 to 30 minutes. When done, remove from the oven and let the polenta stand for 10 to 15 minutes so it sets up. Cut into squares and serve warm.

Variations

* Layer the polenta with the cheeses and tomato sauce and bake; omit the cream.

* Make a middle layer of sautéed artichoke hearts and cover with the cheeses and cream.

* Sauté garlic and mixed greens, such as chard or escarole, in oil until they lose their moisture. Spread the greens between the 2 layers of polenta. You can omit the cheese and cream if you like, adding just a sprinkling of Parmesan on the top.

* Add 1 cup chopped pitted prunes, 2 minced garlic cloves, 2 tablespoons chopped fresh parsley and 1 teaspoon ground cinnamon to 2 cups tomato sauce. Cook together for 10 minutes. Spread half the sauce over the first layer of polenta and half the sauce over the second layer. Top with toasted, skinned, chopped hazelnuts (see page 22), if desired, and bake. Omit the cream and cheeses.

* Sauté wild mushrooms with garlic and parsley in butter and spread them between the 2 layers of polenta. You can omit the cheese and cream if you like, using just a sprinkling of Parmesan on the top.

* Spread sautéed asparagus between the polenta layers or add them to the mushroom mixture.

Corn Fritters *with* Maple Sauce

Serves 4 to 6; makes about 24 fritters

CORN FRITTERS are an old-fashioned New England treat that my father loved as a child on his grandmother's farm. I have added some cornmeal to the typical combination of fresh corn kernels, flour and eggs. The nuggets are deep-fried to a delectable golden brown. My variation on the traditional maple syrup, with which these are usually served, combines the syrup with apple cider and herbs in a light dipping sauce. Serve the fritters for breakfast with sausage, ham or finnan haddie, or as an evening side dish with chowder, roast chicken or turkey, fish, pork, baked ham or browned sausages.

1   cup fresh corn kernels (about 2 ears)

2   large eggs, separated

¼   cup heavy cream

½   teaspoon salt

½   teaspoon sugar

    Freshly ground black pepper

¼   cup cornmeal

¼   cup flour

¼   cup pure maple syrup

1   tablespoon cider or apple juice

1   teaspoon fresh lemon juice

1-2   tablespoons snipped fresh chives

    Corn, vegetable or safflower oil for frying

In a medium bowl, mix the corn kernels, egg yolks, cream, salt, sugar and some pepper. Stir in the cornmeal, then the flour. Let stand for 30 minutes so the starches swell and absorb the liquid.

Meanwhile, make the sauce by combining the maple syrup, cider or apple juice, lemon juice and chives in a small bowl. Set aside.

Pour the oil into a large skillet to a depth of 1 to 1½ inches and heat over medium-high heat.

Beat the egg whites until firm but not dry, and fold into the batter. By tablespoons, drop the batter into the hot oil about 2 inches apart. Fry the fritters in the oil 1 to 2 minutes per side; they should be a deep brown (darker than golden) and crisp.

Drain on paper towels and repeat with the remaining batter. You can keep the fritters warm in a low oven while you fry the rest. Season with salt and pepper just before serving, if desired, and serve with the reserved sauce.

Variations

* For the sauce, change the herb to whatever you like. Try fresh basil, parsley, sage, dill, thyme or marjoram.

* In the fall, I like to replace the maple syrup with reduced cider. To prepare it, bring 1 cup cider to a boil, simmer to reduce it to ¼ cup, add herbs of choice and serve.

Chapter Seven

Rice *and* Beans

EVERY SUMMER at my grandmother's home in Maryland, I feasted on crab cakes, fried chicken with cream gravy, biscuits with sizzled dried beef in cream sauce and, at nearly every meal, rice or cooked white beans. The rice was typically served boiled, but sometimes it was sautéed in a savory pilaf with herbs and butter. The beans were always simmered with greens and a chunk of salty cured country ham.

My grandmother used long-grain white rice. While long-grain has continued to be my staple for boiling, baking or making into pilafs, I've since discovered the joys of rice from other countries and cultures: short-grain from Italy, basmati from the foothills of the Himalayas and chewy brown and wild rice.

Italian short-grain white rice (known as Arborio) is a plump, rounded grain that produces a sticky or creamy dish, depending on the technique you use. Short-grain is essential for risotto, the custardlike specialty of northern Italy. I have intermingled two Mediterranean cultures and their ingredients in a potent Greek Risotto flavored with cinnamon, mint and currants, liberally augmented with lemon juice.

WHITE RICES ARE THE MOST POPULAR and versatile varieties, but it is the hauntingly aromatic white basmati that gives rise to romance and passion in the kitchen. The perfume of basmati is intensely fragrant. The grain is dried and aged in its native northern India, concentrating its flavor. The grains look long, thin and almost fragile, and their delicate taste is suggestive of nuts and flowers. Basmati rice is best boiled or steamed, and you can also use it in baked dishes. One of my all-time favorite ways of preparing it is in a heady oven-baked casserole with browned mushrooms and a savory custard spiced with cardamom. While I eat it for breakfast quite often, it is great with lamb, chicken, fish or for dinner on its own.

With a nutlike savor, brown rice is chewier than white and blends well with toasted nuts and heavier garnishes, such as cheeses. It requires a longer cooking time than white rice—45 to 60 minutes. It may be boiled or used in pilafs. Don't neglect to try the dynamic Marinated Brown Rice Salad with crisp, sweet red peppers, sugar snap peas and black olives.

Like brown rice, wild rice—which is really the seed of an aquatic grass—has an earthy quality that pairs well with mushrooms, onions, spices, nuts and fruits. A sweet-savory blend of toasted hazelnuts and dried blueberries, Wild Rice Crunchy and Blue is just the sort of dish to serve with roast chicken on a winter evening. The universal technique for preparing wild rice is to simmer it gently in water. It doesn't lend itself to steaming or boiling, since it splits easily.

ALL THE RICES ARE DOCILE companions, blending in and getting along with everything else on the plate. Not so dried beans. As my grandmother knew, they demand attention, rather than fitting in quietly, and their robust nature makes them apt companions to heartier foods, enabling these side dishes to stand alone. Beans are a natural in homespun American favorites like succotash, a dish my grandmother appreciated. But they can also go exotic. A mixture of tomatoes, orange and sherry vinegar in Summer Chickpea Salad gives them a Spanish feel. Mixed Bean Salad with Gazpacho Dressing unites the different tastes and textures of black, red and white beans in a snappy dressing. Some beans even make good fritters. When I want a delicious side dish for soup, I turn to Panelle with Sage, a savory pan-fried patty made with chickpea flour.

Beans are versatile, but they do take time to cook and therefore require some planning. (Lentils, which can be ready in only 10 minutes,

are an exception.) Other beans need to be soaked in cold water overnight to rehydrate them before they are cooked. A timesaving method is to bring the beans to a boil in lots of fresh cold water. When they boil, shut off the heat, cover the pan and let sit for one hour. Drain and rinse the beans, and they are ready to cook.

Generally, the larger the bean, the longer the preparation time. Some beans will absorb more water than others, so watch the pot, tasting occasionally to check if they are done and adding water as needed. Season the beans with salt after they have cooked to avoid hardening their proteins; salted beans will not absorb water properly.

For convenience, canned beans are a fine substitute for home-cooked, though their texture is softer and they tend to fall apart more easily. If you have the extra time, do as my grandmother did: Choose dried.

RICE and BEANS

Greek Risotto

Serves 6

I LIKE MIXING TECHNIQUES and ingredients from different cultures. Here, I have taken the flavors of Greek stuffed grape leaves and transformed them into an Italian risotto. Serve with broiled shrimp, or roast chicken, pork or lamb.

¼ cup olive oil
½ cup pine nuts
2 small-medium onions, chopped
   Salt
   Freshly ground black pepper
1 cup Arborio rice (Italian short-grain)
1 teaspoon ground cinnamon
½ cup dark raisins or dried currants
¾ cup fresh lemon juice
3 cups chicken stock, warmed
¼ cup chopped fresh mint or
    1 tablespoon dried
¼ cup chopped fresh parsley

Heat the oil in a small nonreactive saucepan over medium-high heat. Add the pine nuts and cook 3 to 5 minutes, or until golden. With a slotted spoon, transfer the nuts to a plate; set aside.

Add the onions to the oil, along with ½ teaspoon salt and some pepper, and cook, stirring, for about 5 minutes, or until the onions begin to lose their moisture and soften.

Add the rice and cook about 2 minutes, stirring, to toast the rice and heat it through. Add the cinnamon and mix in. Add the raisins or currants and lemon juice and cook, stirring continuously, until the liquid is completely absorbed.

Add ½ cup of the warmed stock and continue cooking, stirring, until all is absorbed. Continue, adding ½ cup warmed stock each time, stirring continuously and reducing the heat to medium if the rice begins to stick to the bottom of the pan. The total cooking time for the rice should be 20 to 25 minutes. Toward the end of cooking, the risotto becomes very creamy and custardlike, not soupy. When all the stock has been added, add the reserved nuts, mint and parsley, correct the seasonings, adding more salt and pepper if needed, and serve.

Variations

* Use this risotto to stuff mushrooms, sweet red peppers or eggplant and bake in the oven until the vegetable is tender.

* There are countless ways to flavor risotto. One of my favorite combinations is browned butter, onion, nutmeg, pumpkin and sage. Add small cubes of pumpkin 15 to 20 minutes before the rice is done and sprinkle the finished dish with Parmesan cheese. Use white wine in place of lemon juice.

* I also make a risotto with butter, onion, white wine and stock, and mix raspberry puree into the finished dish.

Rice Costa Rican Style

Serves 6

THIS IS HOW MY COSTA RICAN NIECE, Ali, loves to eat cooked rice: in a bowl mixed with diced tomato and lemon juice. She enjoys this for breakfast, as a snack or as a side dish. The simplicity of this dish always surprises me. Serve on a hot day.

Salt
1 cup long-grain white rice
2 small-medium tomatoes
     (about ½ pound), cored and diced
2 tablespoons unsalted butter
¼ cup fresh lemon juice,
     or more if desired
   Freshly ground black pepper

Bring a large pot of water to a boil. Add ½ tablespoon salt and the rice and stir. Boil the rice over high heat, stirring frequently to prevent it from sticking to the bottom of the pot, 12 to 15 minutes, or until tender. Drain and rinse with warm water to remove the outer layer of starch until the water runs clear. Drain well and place the rice in a medium serving bowl.

Add the tomatoes, butter, lemon juice and pepper to the rice. Mix well with a fork and taste. Add more salt, pepper and lemon juice if desired, and serve.

Variation

* You can add just about anything to boiled rice, but I love it with salsa; with a mix of garlic, parsley, jalapeño peppers and minced ginger; or with cherries and green olives, as in the Rice Pilaf on the following page.

Rice Pilaf *with* Cherries *and* Green Olives

Serves 4 to 6

THIS IS ONE of those sweet-sour-salty dishes that I love. One morning for breakfast, I spread toasted Italian bread with green olive tapenade. There happened to be some cherry jam on the table. This pilaf was inspired by that spontaneous combination. Serve with duck, pork, chicken, veal or fish.

2   tablespoons unsalted butter
1   medium onion, chopped
    Salt
    Freshly ground black pepper
1   cup long-grain white rice
1¾   cups chicken stock or water, warmed
½   pound fresh sweet cherries,
        such as Bing, pitted and quartered
24   green olives, pitted and quartered

Melt the butter in a medium saucepan over medium heat. Add the onion, ⅛ teaspoon salt and some pepper and cook 3 to 5 minutes, or until the onion begins to lose its moisture and softens.

Add the rice and cook, stirring, to toast the rice and heat it through, 1 to 2 minutes. Add the stock or water, bring to a boil, reduce the heat to low, cover and simmer 15 to 20 minutes, or until all the liquid is absorbed. Remove from the heat and let stand 10 minutes so the rice absorbs the steam in the pan.

Uncover; fluff with a fork. Gently mix in the cherries and olives. Correct the seasonings, adding more salt and pepper if needed, and serve.

Variations

* Add toasted slivered almonds at the end (see page 22).

* Add saffron with the chicken stock or water and toss the rice with toasted slivered almonds at the end.

* Use dried cherries in the winter months.

* Omit the cherries and olives and mix the rice with any of the following combinations:
    steamed asparagus, lemon zest and dill;
    slivered carrots sautéed in butter, toasted pecans
        and sherry;
    sautéed leeks, bacon and parsley;
    sautéed mushrooms and fennel;
    lemon zest and pitted black olives

* Make the pilaf with brown rice. Use 2½ cups liquid and cook for about 45 minutes.

Baked Basmati Rice *with* Cardamom Custard

Serves 6 to 8

THIS AROMATIC CASSEROLE is similar to rice pudding. Cooked rice and browned mushrooms are mixed with a smooth, savory custard flavored with cardamom. If possible, select true Indian basmati rice; Texmati rice does not have the same aromatic quality. Serve with veal, lamb, fish or chicken.

1 cup white basmati rice

3 cups milk

1 tablespoon ground cardamom
  Salt

2 tablespoons unsalted butter

½ pound (1 medium-large) red onion, chopped
  Freshly ground black pepper

1 pound mushrooms, rinsed, trimmed and sliced

3 large eggs

2 cups light cream, half-and-half or milk

1 cup fresh bread crumbs

Combine the rice, 3 cups milk, 1 teaspoon of the cardamom and 1 teaspoon salt in a medium saucepan.

Bring to a boil, reduce the heat to low and simmer, with the cover askew, 20 minutes. Shut off the heat, cover and let stand 10 minutes; the rice will be tender.

Meanwhile, heat the butter in a large skillet over medium heat and add the onion. Sprinkle with salt and pepper and cook about 5 minutes, stirring often, until it loses its moisture and softens. Add the mushrooms and 1 teaspoon of the cardamom, cover, and cook, stirring often, until the mushrooms lose their moisture. Uncover and brown the mushrooms, 10 to 15 minutes. Season with pepper.

Preheat the oven to 375 degrees F.

Place the eggs in a large bowl with some salt, pepper and the remaining 1 teaspoon cardamom. Whisk in the cream or milk and beat until well mixed. Stir in the mushrooms and rice. Transfer to a 13-by-9-inch baking dish and scatter the crumbs over the top.

Bake 30 to 35 minutes, or until the casserole is set and the top is browned. Let stand for 10 minutes so it sets up, then serve.

Variation

* Add sautéed eggplant before baking.

Wild Rice Crunchy *and* Blue

Serves 4 to 6

USING INGREDIENTS native to America, this dish combines cooked wild rice with toasted hazelnuts and dried blueberries for a delectably sweet, savory and crunchy result. Make double the amount of hazelnut butter and freeze any extra so that you have it for another meal; it is delicious on egg noodles, baked polenta, steamed artichokes or sautéed red peppers. Serve this dish with duck, rabbit, venison, chicken, veal or pork.

⅔ cup wild rice (about 4 ounces)

3 cups cold water

Salt

2 tablespoons dried blueberries

¼ cup hazelnuts, toasted and skinned (see page 22)

4 tablespoons unsalted butter, softened

Freshly ground black pepper

Rinse the wild rice well and combine with the cold water and ½ teaspoon salt in a medium saucepan; bring to a boil. Reduce the heat to low, cover and simmer 45 minutes. During the last 10 minutes of cooking, add the dried blueberries.

Meanwhile, make the hazelnut butter. Grind the hazelnuts in a food processor or blender, or chop finely with a knife. Transfer to a bowl and add the butter, a pinch of salt and some pepper. Set aside.

When the rice is done, drain well and transfer to a medium serving bowl. Add as much hazelnut butter as desired and toss with a fork to coat. Taste for seasonings, adding more salt and pepper if needed, and serve.

Marinated Brown Rice Salad

Serves 6

THIS SALAD OF CHEWY BROWN RICE, sugar snap peas, black olives and sweet red peppers is both healthful and pleasing. Dressed with a citrus-spice vinaigrette and surrounded by glistening orange slices, the vibrant medley makes great picnic food and keeps well for three to four days. It is enjoyable with all grilled food, especially fish, chicken and steaks, as well as with stir-fried tofu.

Salt
1 cup long-grain brown rice
¼ cup fresh lemon juice
¼ cup orange juice
1 garlic clove, minced
1 teaspoon dry English mustard
¼ teaspoon ground allspice
¼ teaspoon ground cloves
Freshly ground black pepper
½ cup safflower oil
½ cup olive oil
2 tablespoons heavy or light cream
4 tablespoons chopped fresh parsley
2 navel oranges, peeled

4 ounces sugar snap peas, trimmed and sliced in thirds on the angle
12-24 brine-cured black olives, pitted and halved
½ large sweet red pepper (about ¼ pound), diced

Bring a large pot of water to a boil, add ½ tablespoon salt and the rice and bring back to a boil. Boil the rice over medium-high heat, stirring often to prevent it from sticking to the bottom of the pot, until it is tender, about 45 minutes.

Meanwhile, make the dressing. Place the lemon juice, orange juice, garlic, mustard, allspice, cloves, ¼ teaspoon salt and some pepper in a bowl. Whisk to combine. Slowly whisk in the oils and then the cream. Add the parsley and set aside to allow the flavors to blend.

Using a very sharp or serrated knife, slice the oranges crosswise into circles about ¼ inch thick. Set aside.

When the rice is done, drain and rinse under warm water. Drain well again so there is no remaining water to dilute the dressing. Transfer the rice to a large serving bowl.

Whisk the dressing again to blend it and taste for seasonings, adding salt and pepper if needed. Pour the dressing over the rice. Add the peas, olives and red pepper to the bowl and toss everything together until well mixed. Arrange the orange slices around the outer edge of the bowl. Cover and marinate in the refrigerator for at least 2 to 4 hours. Serve cold.

Sweet-*and*-Sour Grains Pilaf

Serves 6 to 8

THIS IS AN ELEGANT and colorful dish to make when entertaining. The pilaf consists of bulgur, wild rice and white rice. Each grain is cooked separately before being added: The bulgur is softened in warm water, the wild rice is simmered and the white rice is sautéed in butter and simmered. Sweet and sour flavors are added with dried cranberries and blueberries. Serve with poultry, pork, veal, lamb or beef.

½ cup coarse bulgur

1 tablespoon oil of choice,
  such as vegetable or safflower

2½ cups water: ½ cup hot, 2 cups cold

2 tablespoons dried blueberries

2 tablespoons dried cranberries

½ cup wild rice
  Salt

4 tablespoons unsalted butter

1 small onion, chopped
  Freshly ground black pepper

½ cup long-grain white rice

1 cup minus 2 tablespoons chicken
  stock or water, warmed

Place the bulgur in a medium bowl and add the oil. Toss with a fork to coat the grains. Add the ½ cup hot water and dried fruits and stir well. Cover and soak for 1 hour, or until the grains are soft; set aside.

Rinse the wild rice well and place in a small saucepan with the 2 cups cold water and ¼ teaspoon salt. Bring to a boil, reduce the heat to medium-low and simmer 45 minutes, covered.

Meanwhile, melt 1 tablespoon butter in a small saucepan over medium heat. Add the onion and some salt and pepper, and cook about 3 minutes, until the onion loses its moisture. Add the white rice and toss to coat with the butter. Cook for a few minutes until the rice is hot, stirring often. Add the stock or water, bring to a boil, reduce the heat to low, cover and cook for 15 to 20 minutes, or until tender. Remove from the heat and let stand, covered, 10 minutes so the grains absorb the steam in the pan.

When the wild rice is done, drain well and place in a medium serving bowl. Add the bulgur, white rice and the remaining 3 tablespoons butter. Toss well with a fork. Taste and correct the seasonings, adding more salt and pepper if needed, and serve.

Lentil Tabbouleh

Serves 6

YOU CAN BUY THIS in the grocery store, but it is well worth the minimal effort to make your own. Bright with lemon juice, tabbouleh is traditionally made with bulgur and garnished with an abundant amount of chopped parsley and mint. This version substitutes lentils for the bulgur and adds bit of diced tomato. Serve this fresh-tasting dish with lamb, chicken, fish, hamburgers or turkey burgers.

1½ cups lentils
1 bay leaf
1 teaspoon fresh thyme leaves
    or ½ teaspoon dried
    Salt
1 cup chopped fresh parsley
½ cup chopped fresh mint
¼ cup (packed) sliced scallions
3 tablespoons extra-virgin olive oil
    Freshly ground black pepper
½ cup fresh lemon juice
    (about 1½ large lemons)
3 small-medium tomatoes
    (about ½ pound), cored and diced

Place the lentils in a medium saucepan, cover with water, add the bay leaf and thyme and bring to a boil. Simmer over medium heat 10 minutes. Add 1 teaspoon salt and simmer 5 to 10 minutes more, or until tender. Drain, discard the bay leaf, transfer to a medium serving bowl and cool to room temperature.

Add the parsley, mint, scallions, oil, 1 teaspoon salt and lots of pepper. Mix well to coat the lentils with oil. Add the lemon juice and toss to mix. Add the tomatoes and mix in.

Marinate in the refrigerator for 1 to 2 hours. When ready to serve, toss and correct the seasonings, adding more salt, pepper and lemon juice as needed, then serve.

Stewed Fava Beans *with* Spinach *and* Tarragon

Serves 4

THIS IS A QUICK and easy vegetable stew to put together. Fava beans are best when eaten young, when they are about the size of a thumbnail or even smaller. With age and size, their sugars turn to starches and their skins toughen. Their creamy taste and texture is somewhat akin to that of lima beans, yet they are sweeter and more tender. Favas go well with spinach. Serve with ham, sausage, pork and fish.

2 cups shelled fresh fava beans
(1½-2 pounds unshelled)
¼ cup water
2 tablespoons unsalted butter
2 tablespoons chopped fresh tarragon
or 2 teaspoons dried
Freshly ground black pepper
6 ounces spinach leaves, coarsely chopped
Salt

If the fava beans are large, boil them in water for 5 minutes, drain, rinse under cold water and slip off the skins.

Place the beans, water, butter, dried tarragon (if using) and some pepper in a small saucepan. Cover, bring to a boil, reduce the heat to medium-low and simmer until tender, 10 to 15 minutes depending on the size of the beans.

Add the spinach, ¼ teaspoon salt and fresh tarragon (if using), and stew another 5 minutes. Correct the seasonings, adding more salt and pepper if needed, and serve.

Variations

* Stew with artichokes. Add a 10-ounce package frozen artichoke hearts, thawed and trimmed of any tough outer leaves, with the beans.

* You can use other fresh shell beans, such as lima, butter, white or cranberry beans in place of the favas.

Succotash Stew

Serves 6

THIS SUCCOTASH gets a boost of corn taste from the cobs, which are simmered in the cream sauce after the kernels have been scraped off. The cobs are then removed and the limas and corn kernels are cooked until tender.

2 tablespoons unsalted butter

1 medium-large red onion
(about ½ pound), chopped
Salt
Freshly ground black pepper

1½ cups chicken or vegetable stock

1 cup heavy cream

2 tablespoons chopped fresh savory,
sage or thyme or 2 teaspoons dried

3 ears corn, kernels cut off the cob
(2-3 cups), cobs reserved

2 cups shelled baby lima beans
(1½-2 pounds unshelled)
or 2 cups frozen, thawed
Lemon wedges (optional)
Chopped fresh parsley (optional)

Melt the butter in a large saucepan over medium-high heat. Add the onion, ¼ teaspoon salt and some pepper and sauté about 5 minutes, or until the onion begins to lose its moisture and softens. Add the stock, cream, herb of choice and corn cobs. Bring to a boil and lower the heat to medium to achieve a gentle boil. Cook for 25 minutes to flavor the sauce with the corn cobs, turning the cobs in the sauce from time to time if they are not submerged.

Meanwhile, if you are using fresh lima beans, blanch them in boiling water for 5 minutes.

Remove the cobs from the sauce and discard. Add the lima beans and corn kernels, bring to a boil, reduce the heat to low and simmer 10 to 15 minutes more, or until the lima beans are tender and the sauce coats the mixture. Correct the seasonings, adding salt and pepper as needed. Serve with lemon wedges and sprinkle with parsley, if desired.

Variations

* Add cubed, peeled pumpkin along with the lima beans and corn.

* Serve this dish over pasta.

* You can use other fresh shell beans, such as fava, cranberry, butter or white.

Mixed Bean Salad *with* Gazpacho Dressing

Serves 4 to 6

MY FAVORITE SUMMERTIME SOUP is gazpacho. Not only does it incorporate the freshest-tasting produce at its peak, but it is quick to make, low in fat and refreshing. In this recipe, gazpacho is reincarnated as a dressing for an array of black, white and red beans, with parsley mixed in.

Dried beans are essential; the flavor of canned will disappoint. For the gazpacho, a blender produces better results than a food processor.

For the beans

- ½ cup dried red beans
- ½ cup dried white beans, such as white pea
- ½ cup dried black beans
- 1 bay leaf
- 1 teaspoon fresh thyme leaves or ½ teaspoon dried
- 1-2 tablespoons extra-virgin olive oil
- Salt
- Freshly ground black pepper

For the gazpacho

- 1 cup diced ripe tomatoes
- 2 tablespoons chopped red onion, 1 tablespoon cut into chunks and 1 tablespoon into fine dice
- 1 garlic clove, cut into quarters
- ½ cup diced cucumber
- ¼ cup finely diced red or green sweet pepper
- 2 tablespoons chopped fresh parsley
- 2 tablespoons extra-virgin olive oil
- 2 tablespoons red wine vinegar
- Salt
- Freshly ground black pepper
- Tabasco sauce (optional)
- Lettuce leaves for serving (optional)

To cook the beans: Place them in a large bowl, add cold water to cover by 1 inch and soak overnight. Alternatively, place them in a large pot and cover with cold water. Bring to a boil, remove from the heat, cover and let stand for 1 hour. Drain the beans, place in a medium pot, cover with cold water, add the bay leaf and thyme and bring to a boil. Reduce the heat to medium-low and simmer the beans until they are tender, 45 minutes to 2 hours depending on the beans.

Put a layer of paper towels on a cookie sheet or jelly-roll pan. Drain the beans well, remove and discard the bay leaf and transfer the beans to the paper-towel-lined cookie sheet. (Excess water will dilute the gazpacho dressing.) When the beans are dry, transfer to a large serving bowl, add the oil, ¼ teaspoon salt and some pepper and toss together.

Meanwhile, make the gazpacho: Place half the tomatoes in a blender with the onion chunks and the garlic. Blend until the mixture is pureed. Add the cucumber and the remaining tomato and blend just to chop. Transfer to a medium bowl. Add the finely diced onion, sweet pepper, parsley, oil, vinegar, ½ teaspoon salt, some pepper and Tabasco, if using. Mix all together and correct the seasonings, adding more salt, pepper or Tabasco as needed.

When the beans are dry, pour the gazpacho over them and toss well. Marinate in the refrigerator for at least 2 hours or overnight. Before serving, correct the seasonings, adding salt, pepper and Tabasco if needed, and serve either from the bowl or on a bed of lettuce leaves.

Variations

* Top the dish with blanched green and wax beans.

* Use other dried beans, such as chickpeas, kidney, cannellini (white kidney beans) or pinto, or fresh shell beans, such as cranberry, butter, lima or fava beans.

Summer Chickpea Salad

Serves 4 to 6

THIS MARINATED SALAD of chickpeas, corn and tomatoes has a Spanish feel with its dressing of sherry vinegar and orange-scented oil. Serve with lamb chops, chicken legs, shrimp, lobster, salmon, hamburgers, turkey burgers or pork tenderloin.

Orange oil is available in specialty-food shops.

2 cups cooked chickpeas (or substitute a 19-ounce can, rinsed and well drained)

1 cup cooked corn kernels (1-2 ears)

2 medium tomatoes (about ½ pound), cored and diced

¼ cup minced red onion

1-2 tablespoons Dijon mustard

2 tablespoons sherry vinegar
Salt
Freshly ground black pepper

6 tablespoons extra-virgin olive oil

½ teaspoon orange oil or ½ teaspoon grated orange zest

¼ cup chopped fresh parsley or snipped fresh chives

Place the chickpeas, corn, tomatoes and onion in a medium serving bowl. Toss to combine.

In a small bowl, place 1 tablespoon mustard, vinegar, a pinch of salt and some pepper. Whisk to combine. Slowly whisk in the olive oil and orange oil or orange zest. Add the parsley or chives. Taste for seasonings and correct, adding more mustard, salt and pepper if needed.

Pour the dressing over the salad and toss thoroughly. Marinate 1 to 2 hours in the refrigerator, toss, taste for seasonings and add salt and pepper as needed, then serve.

Variations

* Add garlic to the dressing.

* Add diced sweet red pepper to the salad.

* Mix some yogurt into the dressing with the vinegar and mustard.

* This dish can be converted into a stew by cooking the chickpeas with the tomatoes, sherry vinegar, 1 cup white wine, onion, garlic, sweet pepper and the orange oil. Add the corn at the end of cooking and sprinkle the dish with chopped fresh parsley.

Braised White Beans *with* Fennel

Serves 4 to 6

THIS DISH needs long cooking. Make it ahead and reheat at mealtime. Serve with lamb, roast poultry or Italian sausage.

1 cup dried cannellini (white kidney beans)
¼ cup olive oil
1 medium red onion, chopped
2 garlic cloves, minced
  Freshly ground black pepper
1 tablespoon chopped fresh summer
  savory or 1 teaspoon dried
1 quart chicken stock or half water
  and half chicken stock
4 small-medium fennel bulbs or 2 large
  Salt
2 tablespoons fresh lemon juice
2 tablespoons chopped fennel greens
  or fresh parsley
¼ cup diced black olives (optional)

Place the beans in a medium bowl, cover with cold water by 1 inch and soak overnight. The next day, drain and rinse the beans and set aside. For an alternative quick-soak method, see page 147.

Preheat the oven to 325 degrees F.

Heat the oil in a medium skillet over medium-high heat. Add the onion and garlic and sauté 3 to 5 minutes, or until they begin to lose their moisture and soften. Season with pepper and add the savory. Toss well to combine, add the drained beans and mix well. Transfer to a 13-by-9-inch baking dish and add 2 cups stock. Stir gently to combine.

Trim off the stalks of the fennel bulbs and reserve for another use or discard. Cut the bulbs in half lengthwise through the core; remove and discard the cores. Cut each half piece in half again lengthwise and place all the pieces over the beans; press down to nest the pieces in the beans. Add more stock to cover the fennel pieces by half, cover the dish with foil and bake 1 hour. Check the level of stock; add more if necessary to keep the beans moistened as they swell. Bake 1 hour more, or until the beans are tender.

Remove from the oven, uncover and sprinkle with salt, lemon juice and chopped fennel or parsley. Taste for seasonings and serve with chopped black olives, if desired.

Panelle *with* Sage

Serves 4

THESE FLAT FRITTERS made with chickpea flour are served as a snack in Sicily. The batter is prepared like fried polenta, with the flour mixture stirred into boiling liquid, cooked until very thick, cooled, cut into squares and fried. But while polenta has a cornlike taste, panelle is smooth and creamy, with the flavor of chickpeas. Panelle fritters make great accompaniments to soups, especially hearty main-course fish soups. Chickpea flour is available in Italian markets and some health-food stores.

Vegetable, peanut or safflower oil
for cooking
1½ cups chickpea flour
3 cups vegetable stock or water
2 tablespoons extra-virgin olive oil
3 tablespoons chopped fresh sage leaves
or parsley, or 1 tablespoon dried
crumbled
Salt
Freshly ground black pepper
Fresh sage leaves for garnish (optional)

Lightly oil a cookie sheet or jelly-roll pan with sides and set aside.

Place the chickpea flour in a medium bowl and whisk in 1½ cups cold or room-temperature stock or water. Add the olive oil, sage or parsley, ½ teaspoon salt and ½ teaspoon pepper. Whisk well. Bring the remaining 1½ cups stock or water to a boil in a heavy-bottomed medium saucepan. Gradually add the flour mixture, whisking constantly to remove all lumps. Switch to a wooden spoon.

Bring to a boil, reduce the heat to medium and cook, stirring, until very thick, 10 to 15 minutes. Remove from the heat and spread the batter on the prepared sheet in an even layer; cool.

When the mixture has cooled, cut into squares, rectangles or diamonds. Pour oil in a large skillet to the depth of ½ inch. Heat the oil over medium-high heat and fry the fritters in batches until golden on both sides, about 3 minutes per side. Drain on paper, season with salt and pepper and serve with fresh sage leaves as a garnish, if desired.

Chapter Eight

Condiments

I AM PARTIAL TO SWEET AND SOUR, sweet and spicy or sweet and salty taste combinations. I love sugary caramel syrup, cooked until it is mahogany dark and paired with tart rhubarb. Or plump cloves of garlic in a stinging salt and vinegar bath, or pears and raspberries mingling in raspberry vinegar. These condiments and others like them stand in my refrigerator, ready to invigorate boring meals or embellish festive ones.

In condiments, opposites often unite, which accounts for a large part of their allure. The tastes

151

and textures are meant to surprise, astonish and generally make eating a lot more interesting. By nature, condiments are assertive, their flavors animated and alive, their colors vivid and shiny. They light up everyday foods like roast chicken or poached fish. A few others, like raita, a yogurt and cucumber sauce, are soothing, designed to bring relief to a heavily spiced meal.

MOST OF THE CONDIMENTS in this chapter can be served as out-of-the-ordinary side dishes. Many old favorites have been given simple new twists. Classic cranberry sauce, for example, gets a new lease on life from the addition of fresh strawberries. Spiced Cherries, another holiday standout, are poached in a broth of red wine, sweet spices and herbs. Sweet Onion and Berry Relish performs equally well at the side of the plate or on top of a hamburger, like traditional relish.

Other condiments bring together ingredients that are normally strangers to reveal their hidden compatibility. One day, remembering a favorite holiday ham with a crispy mustard and pineapple glaze, I decided to prepare a condiment inspired by the combination. The two turned out to be meant for each other, the succulent fruit blossoming under the sting and heat of the mustard. On another day, it occurred to me to introduce sun-dried tomatoes to dried apricots. They were, I felt, intrinsically similar. After I added tiny onions and fresh mint, which go with both of them, the two got along famously.

Just as I like mixing ingredients, I enjoy serving condiments in unexpected ways. For Chinese food, I always bring out Cranberry and Strawberry Sauce. Rich meats, such as duck, ham or even lamb, receive a blessing of sweet and rich plum jam. Spiced Cherries, delicious with vanilla ice cream, are sensational with lamb, pork or poultry.

LIKE A GOOD STEW, which is after all another marriage of compatibles, all condiments are better when made ahead. Their flavors are absorbed into one another as they develop and mature. Condiments keep well for one to two weeks in the refrigerator—several days longer than most other side dishes. All of the following recipes—compotes and jams, complex chutneys and simple relishes—expand the scope of condiments far beyond ordinary ketchup and mustard.

CONDIMENTS

Cranberry *and* Strawberry Sauce

Serves 6 to 8

EVEN THOUGH STRAWBERRIES and cranberries are not seasonal mates, they taste delicious together. This cranberry combination is one of my favorites; the orange juice creates a nice bridge between the two fruits. I have also made this dish successfully with dried strawberries, but it's not quite the same as with fresh. It is equally spectacular with fresh blueberries.

Cranberries freeze well, so collect a supply in the fall for use throughout the winter and spring months. Serve with roast turkey breast, roast chicken or pork.

1   cup pure maple syrup

1   cup orange juice

1   12-ounce bag fresh cranberries

1   pint fresh strawberries, hulled
       and cut into small wedges

Combine the maple syrup and orange juice in a medium nonreactive saucepan. Bring to a boil over high heat. Add the cranberries and strawberries and return to a full boil, stirring often. Reduce the heat to medium and gently boil for 5 more minutes, stirring often, until the cranberries pop and soften.

Transfer to a medium bowl, cool and chill in the refrigerator. Serve chilled or slightly cooler than room temperature. This sauce keeps well for 1 to 2 weeks in the refrigerator.

Variations

* Make this with 1 pint fresh blueberries instead of the strawberries.

* Substitute 1 package dried strawberries, coarsely chopped, for the fresh strawberries.

* Substitute 1 package dried blueberries for the fresh blueberries or strawberries.

* Use ½ package each dried strawberries and blueberries in place of the fresh fruit. Coarsely chop the dried strawberries.

* Change the maple syrup to sugar or try with a little honey and sugar. Change the orange juice to another juice or water. I have made this with cranberry juice, apple juice and tangerine-orange juice.

* I also make this with dried cherries, both tart and sweet.

Cranberry-Ginger Compote

Serves 6 to 8

CRANBERRIES, APRICOTS AND GINGER make this compote sweet, spicy and tart. It is a huge success at my table. As an alternative to whole-berry cranberry sauce, it goes well with chicken, turkey, pork or even lamb.

2 cups water

1 cup sugar

8 ounces dried apricots, cut into quarters

2 tablespoons minced fresh ginger

1 12-ounce bag fresh cranberries

Place the water, sugar, apricots and ginger in a medium saucepan. Bring to a boil and boil 5 minutes to soften the apricots, stirring often. Add the cranberries, return to the boil, lower the heat to medium and gently boil for 5 minutes more, stirring often, until the cranberries pop and soften.

Remove from the heat and transfer to a medium bowl to cool. Chill and serve. This compote keeps well for 1 to 2 weeks in the refrigerator.

Sweet Onion *and* Berry Relish

Makes 3 to 4 cups

Onions and currants are great partners. Black currant jam provides a deeper, sweeter flavor than dried currants. Serve this with all fish dishes, especially grilled ones, or on duck, chicken, pork, turkey burgers, hamburgers or hot dogs off the grill.

1 pound sweet onions, such as
   Vidalia or Maui, chopped
½ cup black currant or raspberry vinegar
½ cup water
½ cup black currant jam
1 teaspoon salt
   Freshly ground black pepper

Combine all the ingredients in a heavy, medium nonreactive saucepan and bring to a boil. Reduce the heat to medium and simmer briskly 25 minutes, or until the onions are soft and the relish has thickened.

Cool to room temperature, transfer to a medium bowl and chill in the refrigerator. Serve cold. This relish keeps well for 1 to 2 weeks in the refrigerator.

Variations

* Add a spoonful of Cassis (black currant liqueur) when the relish has cooled.

* Add chopped fresh mint after cooling.

Caramel-Rhubarb Chutney

Serves 8 or more

THIS CHUTNEY, a complex union of snappy rhubarb, oranges and raisins, follows the basic formula of cooking all the ingredients together for an hour, but it has the unusual twist of substituting caramel syrup for white sugar.

The chutney improves enormously with an overnight stay in the refrigerator. Serve with broiled swordfish steaks or salmon, shellfish, chicken, lamb, spicy dishes such as curry or Chinese food, and on crackers with Cheddar cheese.

1¼ cups sugar

¼ cup water

Few drops fresh lemon juice

½ cup apple cider vinegar

2 medium oranges, peeled

2 pounds rhubarb, washed, trimmed
and cut into ½-inch slices

1 large onion, chopped

¼ cup (packed) golden raisins

½ teaspoon salt

¼ teaspoon ground cinnamon (optional)

Pinch of cayenne pepper,
or more as desired

Place 1 cup of the sugar in a small nonreactive saucepan with the water and lemon juice. Heat over medium heat, swirling the pan occasionally, until the sugar is dissolved. Do not stir or the syrup may crystallize. Boil until the syrup has turned an auburn color, 5 to 10 minutes.

Remove from the heat and add the vinegar; be careful—the caramel will splatter. Cook over medium heat, whisking to dissolve the caramel, then transfer to a medium nonreactive pan and set aside.

Cut the oranges into ½-inch chunks and add them, with their juice, to the caramel. Add the rhubarb, onion, raisins, salt, cinnamon (if desired), cayenne and remaining ¼ cup sugar. Bring to a boil, lower the heat and simmer briskly for 45 minutes to 1 hour, until thickened, stirring often, so the mixture does not burn.

Transfer to a bowl and cool to room temperature, then refrigerate. The chutney will keep in the refrigerator for up to 3 weeks.

Variations

* Substitute cranberries for the rhubarb and dried strawberries or cherries for the golden raisins.

* Substitute cranberry and apple or pear for the rhubarb.

* Add 1 to 2 tablespoons chopped fresh ginger.

* Add 1 teaspoon or more mustard seeds.

Spiced Cherries

Makes about 4 cups

THIS COMPOTE is an old-time summer favorite. Fresh sweet cherries are simmered in a heady broth of red wine, lemon, sugar, herbs and sweet spices and then chilled in their broth. Although they are delicious with game, ham, pork, sausage, duck, turkey, chicken or lamb, they are also wonderful on vanilla ice cream.

It is worth the money to invest in a cherry pitter for this dish alone. Cherry pitters are inexpensive (between $5 and $10) and can also be used for pitting large olives.

1½ cups dry red wine
1½ cups sugar
2 tablespoons fresh lemon juice
1 strip lemon zest, about 3 x ½ inch
1 bay leaf
1 tablespoon chopped fresh summer savory or 1 teaspoon dried
¼ teaspoon salt
1 teaspoon mustard seeds
1 1-inch piece cinnamon stick
2 whole cloves
¼ teaspoon allspice berries
¼ teaspoon black peppercorns
2 pounds fresh cherries, such as Bing, pitted and halved

In a large nonreactive saucepan, combine the wine, sugar, lemon juice, lemon zest, bay leaf, savory and salt.

Place the mustard seeds, cinnamon stick, cloves, allspice and peppercorns in a piece of cheesecloth and tie the cloth to make a pouch, or place the spices in a tea ball. Add to the pan with the wine mixture.

Bring to a boil and boil 15 minutes. Add the cherries, return to the boil, reduce the heat to medium and simmer briskly with the cover ajar, stirring occasionally, to soften and poach the cherries, about 10 minutes.

Cool to room temperature and remove and discard the lemon zest, bay leaf and the spice package. Transfer the compote to a medium serving bowl. Chill in the refrigerator and serve cold.

Variations

* Substitute orange juice and zest for the lemon.

* Add chopped red onions with the wine.

* Omit the savory and add about 1 tablespoon minced fresh ginger.

* When the cherries have chilled, add a spoonful of Ruby Port or Maraschino liqueur.

Pear and Raspberry Relish

Makes 3 to 4 cups

THIS RELISH is a remarkable fruity-spicy union of chunky pears, whole raspberries and aniseeds. The raspberries are added after the pears have cooked and cooled, so they maintain their shape. Raspberry vinegar adds just enough tartness. This recipe was inspired by one in my friend Kathy Gunst's informative book *Condiments* (G.P. Putnam's Sons, 1984). Serve with chicken, hamburgers or turkey burgers, with rich fish such as salmon or bluefish, or as a side dish with meat sandwiches.

2 Bosc pears, slightly underripe,
    peeled, cored and chopped
⅓ cup sugar or honey
¼ cup raspberry vinegar
2 tablespoons water
2 teaspoons aniseeds
   Salt
   Freshly ground black pepper
½ pint fresh raspberries (about 1¼ cups)
1 tablespoon Framboise or
    Poire William (optional)

Place the pears, sugar or honey, vinegar, water, aniseeds, a pinch of salt and some pepper in a heavy, medium nonreactive saucepan. Bring to a boil, lower the heat and simmer until the relish thickens, about 20 minutes depending on the amount of juice and the ripeness of the pears.

Transfer the relish to a medium bowl and cool to room temperature. When cool, stir in the raspberries and chill in the refrigerator. When it is cold, add the liqueur, if desired. Serve cold. The relish keeps well for up to 2 weeks in the refrigerator.

Italian Prune Plum Jam

Serves 4

YOU CAN MAKE THIS two ways: as a sauce-like compote, which requires less cooking, or as a jam, which cooks for a longer time. Either way, this deep purple jewel looks striking against chicken, turkey, fish, pork or Chinese food.

1¼ pounds Italian prune plums, pitted
½ cup sugar
½ teaspoon ground cardamom
   Salt
3-4 tablespoons fresh lemon juice
   (about 1 lemon)

Combine the plums, sugar, cardamom and a pinch of salt in a heavy, medium nonreactive saucepan. Bring to a boil, reduce the heat to low and simmer for 10 minutes for a compote or 20 minutes for a thicker jam. Transfer to a bowl and cool to room temperature.

Add 3 tablespoons lemon juice to the jam and chill. When cold, taste the jam and add the remaining 1 tablespoon lemon juice, if desired. Serve cold. The jam keeps well for about 3 weeks in the refrigerator.

Variation

* Use fresh apricots in place of the plums in the summer.

Marinated Apricots *and* Sun-Dried Tomatoes

Serves 8

THIS UNUSUAL COMPOTE is as visually pleasing as it is unique. The dried apricots and tomatoes are enhanced by the savory pearl onions and a mint-garlic dressing. Marinate for at least 48 hours so the flavors blend.

The dressing is made in a blender or food processor, but if you do not have either of these appliances, chop the garlic and mint with a knife and whisk into the dressing. Serve with fish and shellfish as well as with chicken and pork.

- 8 ounces dried apricots
- 4 ounces sun-dried tomatoes
- 1 1-pint basket pearl onions, unpeeled
- 1½ cups fresh mint leaves
- 6 garlic cloves, quartered
- ¾ cup fresh lemon juice
  Salt
- 1 cup extra-virgin olive oil
- 1 cup olive oil
  Freshly ground black pepper

Place the apricots in a small saucepan and cover with water. Bring to a boil and boil 1 minute. Drain and rinse with cold water, pat dry and place in a medium bowl. Place the dried tomatoes in a small saucepan and cover with cold water. Bring to a boil. Immediately drain, rinse with cold water, pat dry and add to the apricots.

Bring a medium pot of water to a boil. Add the onions and boil until tender, 10 to 15 minutes depending on size. Rinse under cold water. Using a sharp knife, cut off the root ends and remove the peels; the onions usually pop out. Prick the onions in several places and add to the fruits.

Place the mint, garlic, lemon juice and ½ teaspoon salt in a blender. Blend to chop the mint and garlic. Slowly add the oils. Taste for salt and season with lots of pepper. Pour over the fruits and onions and stir well to coat. Cover and refrigerate for at least 48 hours, stirring occasionally.

To serve, remove the fruits and vegetables with a slotted spoon, leaving just enough dressing to coat. Serve chilled or at room temperature. The compote keeps well for about 2 weeks in the refrigerator.

Variations

* Add 1 to 2 teaspoons fennel seeds to the blender or crush them in a mortar before adding to the dressing.

* Add some grated orange, lime or lemon zest to the dressing. Replace some of the lemon juice with orange or lime juice, to match the zest.

* Add 1 to 2 tablespoons minced fresh ginger to the dressing.

* Substitute a blend of ½ cup fresh tarragon leaves mixed with 1 cup fresh parsley leaves, fairly tightly packed, for the mint.

* Substitute basil leaves (fairly tightly packed) for the mint.

* Use the leftover dressing as a sauce for grilled foods, such as chicken, seafood, steaks or lamb.

Browned Pineapple *and* Mustard

Serves 4

FOR THIS RELISH, pineapple chunks are browned in butter and mixed with grainy and smooth mustards. Chilling mingles the flavors. This recipe uses only half of a pineapple. Or you can double the recipe and use a whole pineapple, since the relish keeps in the refrigerator for about one week. Serve with baked ham or ham steak, kielbasa, chicken, turkey or pork dishes.

1 pineapple, peeled (see page 19),
    quartered lengthwise and cored
1 tablespoon unsalted butter
3 tablespoons smooth Dijon mustard
1 tablespoon grainy Dijon mustard
    Fresh lemon juice to taste (optional)

Cut 2 of the pineapple quarters crosswise into ½-inch slices. (Set aside the rest of the pineapple for another use.) Cut each slice crosswise in half; you will have about 2 cups chunks.

Melt the butter in a large nonreactive skillet over medium-high heat. Add the pineapple chunks in a single layer and brown well, 1 to 2 minutes per side. Reduce the heat to low and cook 10 to 15 minutes until softened and tender, stirring often. Transfer to a medium bowl and cool to room temperature.

Add the mustards, mix well to coat the pineapple and marinate in the refrigerator 1 to 2 hours to blend the flavors. Taste and add lemon juice, if desired. Serve cold.

Pickled Whole Garlic Cloves

Makes about 2 cups

WHEN I FIRST TRIED these at the Fancy Food Show in New York City a few years ago, I was captivated by the softness of the cloves mingling with the pungent brine. The cloves are easy to prepare, but they do require a 48-hour marination period. Use a mild vinegar with no more than 4.5 percent acidity; rice vinegar is a good choice because of its gentle flavor. Serve with pâté, sandwiches, turkey, burgers, chicken or in a martini.

4   large garlic heads (about 12 ounces total), cloves gently crushed and peeled

1½ cups rice vinegar (4-4.5% acidity) Several sprigs fresh thyme, basil, mint, tarragon or parsley or 1-2 teaspoons dried herb of choice

½   teaspoon whole black peppercorns

1   bay leaf

1   teaspoon sugar (optional)

½   teaspoon salt

Bring a medium nonreactive pot of water to a boil, add the garlic cloves, return to the boil, reduce the heat to low and simmer for 3 minutes. Drain the garlic and return it to the pot.

Add the vinegar, herbs, peppercorns, bay leaf, sugar (if using) and salt. Stir and bring back to a boil. Boil for 5 minutes. Pour the mixture into a medium bowl and let it cool to room temperature. When cool, transfer to a bowl with a cover or a glass jar with a lid.

Refrigerate the garlic and let it marinate for 48 hours. Store in the refrigerator. Serve cold like pickles.

Variation

* You can use the leftover vinegar from the pickled cloves as part of a salad dressing, removing the bay leaf first.

Coconut-Ginger Raita

Serves 4 to 6; makes about 1 ⅓ cups

RAITA IS A SAVORY Indian yogurt side dish served to temper the heat of spicy food. It is believed that the word derives from *rai*, meaning black mustard seeds, since that spice is a common ingredient in most raitas. Many combinations can be added to the yogurt, the most well-known being mint, garlic and cucumber. In this version, I've used coconut, garlic and lots of ginger for punch. I like to drain the yogurt a little bit so the dish is thick and less acidic, but it will be refreshing with undrained yogurt. Serve with chicken, lamb, fish, turkey, curry and other spicy dishes.

Black mustard seeds are smaller and spicier than the more common yellow ones. If you can't get the black, substitute brown, which are equally intense and available in many supermarkets and health-food stores.

1½ cups plain whole-milk yogurt

¼ cup chopped unsweetened coconut (available in health-food stores)

1 tablespoon (packed) minced peeled fresh ginger

1 large garlic clove, minced

½-1 teaspoon black or brown mustard seeds, crushed (optional)

Salt

Freshly ground black pepper (optional)

Place a strainer over a small bowl and line it with a paper towel. Place the yogurt in the strainer and set aside to drain for 30 minutes to 1 hour, until you have 1 cup thickened yogurt.

Discard the liquid and transfer the yogurt to the small bowl by rolling it out of the towel and scraping any extra off with a rubber spatula. Add the coconut, ginger, garlic, ½ teaspoon mustard seeds (if using), ¼ teaspoon salt and some pepper, if desired. Mix well and refrigerate until ready to serve. Taste and add more salt and mustard seeds, if desired. The raita keeps well for 1 to 2 weeks in the refrigerator.

Variations

* Add 1 small jalapeño pepper, minced, to the raita.
* Experiment using your favorite fruit, vegetable, herb or spice. Some of my favorites are bananas, cooked potatoes, diced tomatoes, toasted nuts (see page 22), minced scallions or fresh herbs.

Maple Mustard

Makes about ¾ cup

THIS VARIATION ON HONEY MUSTARD takes about 30 seconds to make. It is good served over pan-fried or grilled pineapple (page 19) or grilled bananas (page 18) or with chicken, salmon, ham or pork.

½ cup Dijon mustard, smooth or grainy, or both combined
3 tablespoons pure maple syrup
1 tablespoon fresh lemon juice
   Freshly ground black pepper

Place the mustard in a small bowl. Whisk in the maple syrup, lemon juice and pepper. Set aside at room temperature or in the refrigerator for 1 to 2 hours to allow the flavors to blend. Serve at room temperature or chilled. The mustard keeps for up to 3 weeks in the refrigerator.

Variation

* Add chopped fresh herbs such as thyme, marjoram, parsley, sage or summer savory.

Index

About the Author

DEIRDRE DAVIS WROTE *A Fresh Look at Saucing Foods* (Addison Wesley), which was nominated for a Julia Child Award. Her articles have appeared in *Bon Appétit*, the *Boston Globe* and the *Washington Post*.